Making Capitalism Fit for Society

For Joan

Making Capitalism Fit for Society

Colin Crouch

polity

First published in 2013 by Polity Press
Reprinted, 2015
Polity Press
65 Bridge Street
Cambridge CB2 1UR, UK

Polity Press
350 Main Street
Malden, MA 02148, USA

ISBN-13: 978-0-7456-7222-9 (hardback)
ISBN-13: 978-0-7456-7223-6 (paperback)

A catalogue record for this book is available from the British Library.

Typeset in 11 on 13 pt Sabon
by Toppan Best-set Premedia Limited
Printed and bound in the USA by Edwards Brothers Malloy, Inc.

The publisher has used its best endeavours to ensure that the URLs for external
websites referred to in this book are correct and active at the time of going to
press. However, the publisher has no responsibility for the websites and can
make no guarantee that a site will remain live or that the content is or will
remain appropriate.

Every effort has been made to trace all copyright holders, but if any have been
inadvertently overlooked the publisher will be pleased to include any necessary
credits in any subsequent reprint or edition.

For further information on Polity, visit our website: www.politybooks.com

Contents

Preface

Income inequality in the United States of America has reached such an extreme point that there are fears that it may damage the economy. These views are not just expressed by the 'progressives' who might be expected to have such opinions, but by the International Monetary Fund (IMF) and the Organization for Economic Co-operation and Development (OECD). This is a striking development, for three reasons.

First, the IMF and OECD are usually associated with orthodox economic opinion, which is either indifferent to inequality or, rather, favours it. Indifference is usually expressed in the cliché, 'A rising tide lifts all boats', meaning that if the rich are doing well, then the economy is doing well, so everyone gains and it does not matter if some gain more than others. Behind that usually lies an opinion favourable to increasing inequality, in the belief that growth happens when entrepreneurs have strong incentives to innovate and invest. Something extraordinary is taking place if experts at organizations like the IMF and OECD have started to fear that any such effect is now being undermined by the squeeze operating on moderate and lower incomes, while those of the wealthy, especially in the financial sector, continue to rise.

Second, despite these fears, the political and economic elites of most countries in the developed world remain committed to pursuing the same neoliberal policies that have produced this harmful situation. The USA may have been the global leader in the new inequality, but it is being widely imitated. Almost everywhere, inequality is rising, welfare states are being cut back, trade unions are declining in importance, employee rights are shrinking. At the same time, ever more public resources are devoted to saving the banking system that produced the financial crisis. Those who receive their incomes through financial speculation are being protected and become richer, while those who do so by working at more productive activities are having an ever tougher time.

The third striking fact is that these negative developments are not produced by ineluctable forces beyond human control, but are the results of political choices. True, certain more or less unavoidable factors in the global economy do not make it easy to avoid increasing inequality; but that makes it even more remarkable that so many political decisions gratuitously intensify rather than counter such trends. In particular, recent changes in taxation in most countries have tended to favour those on high incomes, whose pre-tax incomes have also been rising the most strongly. There are alternatives, not in the sense of utopian possibilities, but in real existing examples that we can see around us. However, these examples are themselves now being threatened by the onward march of anti-egalitarian orthodoxy.

These fears of the international organizations provide a remarkable check to the usual claim of anti-egalitarians, that those who complain about inequality are primarily motivated by 'envy'. But there is another, equally powerful argument against that claim. While inequality of wealth does not necessarily hurt those outside the ranks of the rich, its political consequences do. If wealthy interests are able to convert wealth into political power – as is very often the case – they are able to distort both the market economy and democracy. That is a major preoccupation of this book. The collapse of the Soviet Union made it clear, if it was not already, that capitalism is the only complex system known to us that can provide an efficient and innovative economy. But the financial crisis has revealed the potentially pernicious workings of some aspects of capitalism, its dependence on the state to rescue it at public expense from its own contradictions, and the growing inequalities that its elites seems to demand. All this creates reasonable doubt whether social and political arrangements can simultaneously provide a decent life for all citizens and satisfy capitalists' demands. Fortunately, during its history capitalism has shown a flexibility and adaptability that has enabled it to be compatible with several different kinds of society. This is one of the main characteristics that marked its superiority to Soviet communism. But it does not necessarily do this. Everything depends on the balance of power among diverse social and political interests, an imbalance that may leave (as today seems to be the case) capitalist interests dictating terms to the rest of society, but which, under other circumstances, may also enable other interests to exact compromises from them, as was the case in many Western countries during the heyday of the mid-twentieth-century welfare state.

Those compromises were mainly linked to the political force known as social democracy, associated with labour movements and worker-based parties, trade unions and various kinds of worker rights; more widely, with the impact that this movement, and also in some countries communism, had on other, rival political forces. Yet we do not find social democratic parties today confidently asserting a superiority of their approach, despite growing dissatisfaction with many aspects of capitalism. They are mainly to be found on the defensive, pessimistic and feeling themselves left behind by history. This is partly testimony to the overwhelming dominance of neoliberal orthodoxy, but partly because the social democratic vision requires some major adjustments if it is to assert its claim to be the alternative that can challenge that orthodoxy, reshaping capitalism so that it is fit for society, and presenting itself convincingly as a coherent actor or

party allied to economic change and innovation rather than
offering only defensive protection from them. These are,
however, adjustments, radical though they are, that should
be within the reach of the social democratic tradition.

The aim of this book is to argue both why social democracy has this potential, and what adjustments it needs to
make. These are a matter, partly of adopting new positions
on change and innovation, of embracing stronger alliances
and mergers with environmentalist and other new critical
movements, but partly of recognizing and tackling the political power of accumulated wealth that is the negative result
to which neoliberalism has brought us.

In two previous books, *Post-Democracy* (2003) and *The
Strange Non-Death of Neoliberalism* (2011), I have tried to
describe the problems presented to egalitarian democracy by
recent developments in the global economy, and to look for
the ways in which ordinary people might try to cope with
and confront them. Many readers and reviewers have criticized me for offering little more than participation in citizens' initiatives, consumer movements and conscientious
professional organizations with which to confront economic
power. Where is my alternative strategy? My approach
seemed sensible to me, as the number of one's readers who
stand no chance of being able to do anything more than offer
minor challenges vastly outweighs the one or two who might
get anywhere near political strategy. So many books about
politics spend their time exhorting political leaders who will
never notice anything they say, talking right past their actual
readers, who can do very little more about public events than
cope with them. But my critics are right. One must always,
following Antonio Gramsci, be a pessimist with the intellect
but an optimist for the will. While to be naively optimistic
is to experience repeated defeat and eventual disillusion, to
be guided only by the pessimistic expectations that a scientific examination of reality often brings is to experience the
inevitable defeat that comes from never having tried.

This book therefore departs from my others in moving to
examine the real possibilities that exist for creating a better

world than that which is being offered by the wealthy elites who dominate our public and private lives.

To make the book accessible to general readers I have not cluttered the text with bibliographical references. A list of works referred to follows each chapter.

This book is published in German as *Jenseits des Neoliberalismus, Ein Plädoyer für soziale Gerechtigkeit*. Vienna: Passagen Verlag, 2013.

Acknowledgements

Several of the ideas in this book were first tried out in some public lectures that I gave during 2011 and 2012. I am grateful to those attending for questions and comments that helped me sharpen my ideas, though obviously none of them necessarily shares all or even any of the views I have expressed here:

- My valedictory lecture at the University of Warwick, 2 November 2011, 'What remains of a public realm in a privatized society?' I am grateful for ideas from the colleagues who participated in the subsequent conference on 'Beyond the Public Realm': John Bennington, Dorothee Bohle, Wyn Grant, Jean Hartley, Guglielmo Meardi, Paul Marginson, Glenn Morgan, Andreas Rasche, Ralf Rogowski, Philippe Schmitter, Wolfgang Streeck, Jonathan Tritter, Jelle Visser, Noel Whiteside.
- A lecture in the Ralph Miliband Memorial series at the London School of Economics and Political Science, 1 March 2012, 'Social democracy as the highest form of liberalism'.
- The 2012 Cesare Alfieri lecture at the Facoltà di Scienze Politiche, University of Florence, 26 April

2012, 'Europa e problemi della mercatizzazione: da Polanyi a Scharpf'.

- The 2012 annual LEQS lecture at the European Institute of the London School of Economics and Political Science, 28 May 2012, 'A European asymmetry: making markets and dealing with their externalities'.

- A separate paper on 'Social democracy as the highest form of liberalism' presented at a conference on 'The next centre-left century: Lost or anew? American progressive-liberalism and European social democracy', organized by Policy Network and the Foundation for European Progressive Studies at Nuffield College, Oxford, 3 July 2012.

I also learnt a good deal that has been helpful in writing the book by my participation from 2009 to 2012 with excellent colleagues in the EU Framework Programme 7 project 'The Governance of Uncertainty and Sustainability: Tensions and Opportunities' (GUSTO) (contract nr 22530). Of course, any information or views I have drawn from the project are mine only, and do not necessarily reflect those of my colleagues, nor do they in any way represent the official opinion of the European Commission.

My final text has benefited from some very helpful criticism of an earlier version by Philippe Schmitter, John Thompson and anonymous referees at Polity and Passagen Verlag – though of course none of them necessarily thinks I have made a sufficient number of improvements.

I am grateful to my wife, Joan, for contributing to the ideas set out here in our endless, forty-five-year-long conversation, and for pointing out to me the many places in my original text where I failed to communicate clearly. Whether she did this enough, individual readers will have to judge.

1

From a Defensive to an Assertive Social Democracy

European social democracy needs to be shaken out of the defensive posture to which it has shrunk for several years now. It should not be in this position at all. Inequality is again becoming a major issue; the power of large corporations is producing a growing number of problems for consumers, workers and citizens; the neglect of collective needs is producing frightening problems of environmental damage. These are all areas where social democracy has strong positions, and where neoliberal capitalism is at its most vulnerable. We need to understand the paradox whereby, despite this, social democrats in most countries seem depressed, while neoliberals are triumphant; and to explore the changes that social democratic politics needs if it is to move out of defensiveness and reassert itself – alongside environmental and other cause groups – in a new alliance, more integrated than in mere red–green electoral coalitions.

Strictly speaking, the opposite of defensive is offensive; but to talk of an 'offensive social democracy' could well be misunderstood. The same would apply to 'aggressive'. However, feminists have told us that, where men are aggressive, women are assertive. The ancient Greek word *demokratia* having been a feminine noun, she and her various adjectival sisters (social, Christian, liberal, democracy) can therefore claim only to be becoming assertive when they take an offensive position. Hence, I shall speak here of the need for assertive social democracy. If a political movement is to move from defensiveness to assertiveness, it has to find new, forward-looking interpretations of its historical vision, and has to demonstrate that it is the force most capable of bringing valuable innovation to society at large.

I am using 'social democracy' in its normal contemporary sense to describe political movements and parties that have as their historical mission the representation of normal working people, including, prominently, trade unions, by seeking major changes in the operation of a capitalist economy and the inequalities and social damage that they perceive it to produce. The parties are named variously Social Democratic, Labour or Socialist, but 'social democracy' has come to be used as something distinct from 'socialist'. Socialist movements are usually seen as seeking entirely to replace the capitalist economy and markets by a system of common ownership, meaning either the state or a cooperative arrangement. Social democrats, in contrast, accept the market and private ownership as the best means of conducting most economic business, but are deeply sceptical of the market's capacity unaided to achieve certain fundamental social goals. These goals concern: first, the need for all people to be able to enjoy a decent life, even if they cannot be very successful in the market, and with limited inequalities; and second, the need for human beings to be able to manage successfully certain shared, collective tasks. Social democrats are those politically active people who are willing to place constraints on and to shape the market mainly, though not solely, through the use of state or local government power, and in particular through the provision of public services as rights of citizenship, in order to realize those ends.

To repeat the opening paragraph in more detail: modern Western society has extraordinary collective needs and interdependencies. Climate change and other environmental problems, many of them products of our way of life, are threatening that way of life itself, unless we can come together to find solutions. Our economies and societies are increasingly interdependent, bound together as we are through the globalized exchanges of goods, services and financial flows. These interdependencies appear as competitive national rivalries, but in trade the continued success of any one human group is usually improved by the success of everyone else. Sophisticated economies also need advanced infrastructures – transport and communications networks, resources of skilled labour, shared regulatory standards – that depend on collective effort. Western societies are also (in general) rich and can afford to do something about these collective issues while also leaving the great majority of individuals with well-provided private lives. But our societies are also becoming increasingly unequal, decreasingly willing to produce public goods or cover collective risks, while the products of increasing wealth reward an ever smaller minority.

Such a world might be expected to be highly receptive to the messages of social democracy. But, paradoxically, the dominant political ideology – neoliberalism – is leading public policy ever further in exactly the opposite direction: towards increasing attention to purely individual needs, especially those of a privileged elite, to the neglect of both collective ones and the concerns of the great majority. Further, still paradoxically but less surprisingly, our increasing global interdependence is accompanied by growing xenophobia and suspicion of strangers. Although in principle neoliberalism and xenophobia should be mutually incompatible, they appear as allies in many important right-of-centre individual parties or coalitions of parties in contemporary politics.

The answer to these paradoxes is found in the fact that the logic of politics is the logic of power, not that of the coherence of arguments. The contemporary logic of power has several components. I have written in more detail about this in my books *Post-Democracy* and *The Strange Non-Death of Neoliberalism*. I shall here just summarize the

argument. One of the first consequences of economic globalization was to give the investors of capital increased
choice over the parts of the world in which they could place
their investments. Workers in the existing industrial countries found themselves competing for work with those in far
poorer ones, where labour and social costs, business taxation and the provision of public services were far lower, but
where production could now be profitably coordinated from
headquarters in the advanced world.

Similarly, governments in the industrial world found their
countries competing as investment locations with those
whose governments offered investors the attractive features
of lower tax rates, less regulation and bad labour conditions.
This problem is not as overwhelming as it initially seems.
For some activities, firms need the high-quality infrastructures and skilled labour forces that only countries with
strong collective policies and high tax rates can provide – as
we shall later see, an important component of the case for a
confident, assertive social democracy. Also, after a time globalization means that at least some people in poorer countries begin to earn enough to start buying goods and services
from the existing wealthy parts of the world. This is a
process that has already begun, as, for example, Chinese
customers buy German capital goods, British cars and Italian
shoes. Nevertheless, the initial shock of globalization was to
shift the balance of bargaining power between international
investors on the one hand and nationally rooted governments and working classes in the advanced world on the
other. This is where the ostensibly illogical alliance of neoliberalism and xenophobia found its rationale: neoliberalism
wants unfettered global markets; if mass populations are
engaged in mutual suspicion and intolerance, they are also
unlikely to accept the transnational regimes that are the only
institutions that might regulate these markets.

Second, along with this kind of globalization came the
deregulation of financial markets. As we now know, this led
investment bankers to develop a range of highly risky investment strategies that made a very small number of people very

rich indeed, but at the expense of destabilizing the entire global economy. The consequence was the Anglo-American financial crisis of 2008. This did not, however, bring the system of unregulated, high-risk finance to an end. So dependent have we become on the banking system that governments had to rescue banks from the difficulties in which they had put themselves, often meeting the costs by making cuts in social spending. Thus the poor were called upon to bail out the super-rich. Governments also encouraged banks to return to their earlier irresponsible behaviour, but with greater moderation, so that they might become solvent again. When it was being successful, the unregulated finance model was used to demonstrate that banks and markets together could resolve many of the world's economic problems, and that therefore social democracy's approach of regulated markets and strong social policy was not *needed*. Once the model had failed, the need to set it on its feet again was used to demonstrate that social democracy's approach could not be *afforded*. Heads, neoliberalism won; tails, social democracy lost.

Third, and pre-dating both these changes in contemporary capitalism, a major change had been taking place in the support base of social democracy. This had originally rested in the manual working class of manufacturing industry – in particular its male members. The entry into citizenship of this class represented the first moment in the history of organized societies when the mass of ordinary working people had been permitted to play such a role. It provided supporters for policies that recognized the limits of the free market if such people were to have a chance of having secure and decent lives. This class formed trade unions, cooperative movements, and socialist, social democratic and labour parties. But, starting in northern Europe and the USA from the early 1970s onwards, it started to decline in both absolute and relative size. Constantly improving productivity in manufacturing was reducing the need for large numbers of industrial workers; the early stages of globalization were shifting much manual work in manufacturing to the newly developing economies; and demand for various kinds of services increased, generating a different kind of work force. A major part of this new work force was engaged in producing public services: health and other forms of personal care, education, policing and security, public administration. These provided a new support base for social democracy, as the growth of public services was largely championed by social democrats. In particular it provided social democratic parties with female supporters, the majority of public-service jobs being held by women. The private services sectors proved more intractable, not because workers in those sectors were strongly attracted by other parties and forces, but because they have tended not to generate any strong political profile at all. This might seem to present an equal problem to all parties, but as the force that is challenging the main distribution of power in the economy, social democracy needs a positive, strongly identified support base. It is therefore affected asymmetrically by a general decline in political identity, compared with parties representing interests whose strength lies in the market and the economy themselves.

By the early twenty-first century both social democracy's support bases had been put on the defensive. The manual working class continued its irreversible decline, and public employees had been vilified by neoliberal politicians and publicists as parasites living off the taxes of hard-working people in the private sector. If money spent on public services can be portrayed (as it is in much neoliberal rhetoric) as money that might as well be placed in a hole in the ground, then what is to be said of the people who derive their income from putting it in the hole?

Conservative political interests face a major problem in democracies: how can forces which are designed mainly to protect the interests of the privileged attract the support that they need of a majority of people in the middle ranks of society? For much of the nineteenth and twentieth centuries part of the answer (alongside appeals to nationalism) was to point to the masses of property-less workers and paupers and argue that they would, in their envy, attack the property of the lower middle classes as much as they would that of the rich. By the late twentieth century the property-less masses had shrunk to a tiny group, communism had collapsed and the old fears were no longer plausible. Conservative demonology had to invent new menaces. It has done this partly by representing the welfare state as something that takes money from the pockets of all working people, rich and poor alike, in order to give it to those who refuse to work, particularly to foreigners who have come into a country to take the jobs of natives (which they seem to achieve while also refusing to work). Public employees are then an additional menace, working inefficiently and on excessive incomes and with excessive security while busily expediting these transfers to the undeserving. Where socialist and social democratic politicians had once been depicted as the people leading the attack on all property ownership, they are today seen as those who, for reasons that are never really explained, want to engage in this transfer of funds to the feckless and foreign.

In reality, many contemporary social democratic parties have been off on a different path. As their two key constituencies – manual workers and public employees, and the trade unions that flourished only in these sectors – became problematic, many began to suspect that core constituencies, or historically reliable support bases, were not such a good thing to have after all. This produced the 'Third Way' of the British Labour Party, the *Neue Mitte* of the German SPD, the US New Democrats and several others. Social democracy completed its journey to becoming a movement seeking electoral support from anywhere in the society, and financial support mainly from corporate donors, for a general, class-less project of 'progressive reform'. It also abandoned any attempt at changing the political culture of the wider society, just trying to fit in with what market research told it were the prejudices of the existing culture. 'Progressive reform' had been a rallying cry of the liberal and later socialist left of the nineteenth century facing the deeply entrenched and often incompetent institutions of those who had been privileged over the centuries. It now became interestingly ambiguous. It referred to a need to rebuild and improve public services that had been neglected by conservatives pursuing low-tax agendas, but the working habits of the public employees delivering and organizing those services were equally seen as problematic, and in particular the trade unions that represented them. Third Way social democratic parties therefore ceased to say anything problematic about concentrated corporate wealth or even inequality.

These social democrats became first embarrassed at their old supporters, and then disconnected from and increasingly cynical about them. Occasionally one hears social democratic politicians talking about a need to 'reconnect' with their 'core constituency'. This rarely means returning to combating social inequalities; but is a code for a perceived need to be xenophobic, a need that their other constituency of public service professionals, they complain, tries to prevent them from meeting. They also feel themselves doomed to be curators of a political museum, protecting from the rude energies of the dynamic neoliberal world the decaying remains of exhibits labelled 'trade unions', 'labour rights', 'universal health service', 'social citizenship'.

The Problems of Neoliberalism

The despondent state of social democracy does not mean that neoliberalism is enjoying great success – that is, in the real world of practice, as opposed to that of ideology. Not only has it experienced the great check of the 2008 crisis, but its absolutely central claim to popular appeal – that it replaces state command and control by consumers' free choices in the market – is increasingly revealed to be a sham. It is this characteristic that is today leading to legitimate doubt whether capitalism can be made fit for society, or whether it will reshape society to meet its own demands. Actually existing political neoliberalism, as opposed to the models of economics textbooks, is about enhancing the power of great corporations and wealthy individuals. This problem is general across several sectors of the economy, as is explored in detail in a recent book by Stephen Wilks on *The Political Power of the Business Corporation.* It is, however, seen particularly clearly in the response to the financial crisis described above.

In addition, waves of privatization of public facilities and services that have been its central hallmark have similarly served corporate interests. Initially applying only to certain public utilities, privatization is today principally about outsourcing public services to private firms. The state usually remains the paymaster; and usually only a small number of firms is involved in the sub-contracting. Recipients of the services are therefore not customers in the true sense of the word, only users. There is therefore no true market here, just a series of deals between public officials and corporate representatives.

Outsourcing is justified on the grounds that it brings competition, the fundamental condition of a functioning market, but the amount of competition is usually very low. In the case of water supply it is virtually zero, as it has not yet been possible to find means of having more than one company provide water from a particular river basin. In other cases very small numbers of firms engage in very limited competition. It mainly takes place at the stage of winning contracts, the contract itself frequently entailing monopoly supply rights for a number of years. This is the case, for example, with contracting out school, health and social care services. To achieve stability of supply and avoid frequent disruption, contracts have to be set for long periods, often up to twenty-five years. During that prolonged interval there is no competition at all. When contracts are eventually re-tendered, there is a strong – though not universal – presumption in favour of renewal by the incumbent firm; its managers will have developed strong relations with public officials involved in the negotiations; and upheaval can be avoided by staying with an existing supplier.

Outsourcing is also justified on the grounds that private firms bring new expertise, but an examination of the expertise base of the main private contractors shows that the same firms keep appearing in different sectors. For example, the UK-based but globally active firm SERCO has contracts in all sectors of transport (including air traffic control), prisons and security, the management of privatized government research centres, leisure centres, defence and schools. Similar accounts can be given of other firms in several other countries. The expertise of these corporations, their core business, lies in knowing how to win governments contracts, not in the substantive knowledge of the services they provide. For the latter task they depend on re-recruiting people already working in the field – normally in the public sector organizations from whom they have won the contracts. This explains how and why they extend across such a sprawl of activities, the only link among which is the existence of a government contract-winning process. Typically these firms will have former politicians and senior civil servants on their boards of directors, and will often be generous funders of political parties. This too is part of their core business. It is very difficult indeed to see how ultimate service users gain anything from this kind of politically managed competition.

A further claim made for outsourcing is that it drives costs down. It is difficult to understand why this might be so, given the limited nature of competition, the cosy nature of the relations between contractors and public officials, the need for private firms to make enough profit to please their shareholders, and the transaction costs involved when a service moves from being provided in-house to being contracted out. There is however one area where there seem to be important cost savings: private firms are able to pay low wages and maintain poor working conditions for their lower levels of staff. Public authorities on the other hand have to maintain some reputation for being 'good' employers, or they face public criticism. And if there is scandal about the treatment of staff by firms, the political flak is usually borne by the public authorities that gave them the contracts rather than the firms themselves. In the UK, some contractors have been paying wages so low that their employees receive publicly funded subsidies to their wages from a government tax credit scheme. The low wages enable the contractors to claim that granting them the contracts saved public money, but another part of the public funds bears the burden of the tax credits; overall it is doubtful if any public money is saved.

Finally, outsourcing and other forms of involvement of private firms in public business are justified on the grounds that they enable governments to share the financial risks of large projects with private investors. The investors will make a profit if the project works well, and a loss if it does not, exactly as the capitalist market is supposed to work. The principal examples here are the public–private funding partnerships used to fund large infrastructure projects and school and hospital building programmes. Typically, a private investment firm undertakes the capital cost of a public programme, in exchange owning the public asset being created (for example, a hospital). It then leases the asset back to the public service concerned, which repays the capital investment over a long period. But the contract terms bind the public service to a particular pattern of use, which can impose major rigidities over the years as the service's needs change. More importantly, following the 2008 financial crisis, we now have a number of examples where the risk element of capital funding has become real. Invariably, central governments have moved in to underwrite the risks and guarantee the private investors' return – taking us back to where governments stood in relation to public investment projects in the first place, a position from which the shared investment with the private sector was supposed to rescue them. This is an example of a far more general problem. In economic theory capital bears the risk of economic enterprise, and the interest it earns reflects that risk. However, in the changed power balance between investors on the one hand and employees, governments and wider societies on the other, capital is frequently able to demand a secure rate of return, throwing risk on to the other participants.

Really strict theories of neoliberalism see very little role for the state at all, as we see most clearly in the demands for very limited government by the US Republican Party. But this is unrealistic, and bears little relation to the reality of neoliberalism itself. Societies, especially complex modern ones engaged in sophisticated economic activities, need governments. Lacking a coherent theory of a relationship between government and economy because of their primitive anti-government stand, neoliberals have therefore produced an astonishing sleight of hand. By not distinguishing between markets and corporations, they are able to claim that placing something in the hands of corporations is the same as placing it in the market. These corporations, in turn, then form close relations with public officials. The fiction is maintained even though, as is usually the case, the very characteristics of the market of which boasts are made – like choice by ultimate consumers, an absence of political interference by business interests and risk-bearing by capital – are all missing. At best there is deception; at worst outright corruption. Neoliberalism in this particular form is becoming a highly dubious political force. And yet this is the dominant political ideology, which, it is widely claimed, has seen social democracy off the historical stage.

Sadly, one reason why social democrats have been unable to profit politically from the hypocrisy of neoliberalism's relations with large corporations is that governments led by social democratic parties have been implicated with others in allowing and even encouraging this pattern of relations between governments and firms to develop. This has been partly for the worst of reasons; social democratic politicians have been among those who have taken the corporate shilling and occupied places on the boards of corporations seeking public contracts. But there have also been more honourable motives. If many major banks had collapsed in 2008, the worst casualties would have been among ordinary people with slender financial resources, unable to protect themselves from disaster. The simplest approach to the crisis, and one with which the banks could be relied upon to cooperate, was to compensate them for their own irresponsible risks, and then to hope that they would become profitable again as quickly as possible. But the only way they know to do this is to return to the risky practices that caused the problem in the first place.

Similar arguments apply to the privatization and outsourcing of public services. Education, health care, pensions and social insurance, transport, public utilities are all services for which modern societies have very high and predictable demands. At a time when much manufacturing and some services activities are subject to competitive pressures from globalization, they represent some of the remaining sectors where profits might still be made within the advanced world. Corporations therefore dearly want a share in their provision, but this can only happen if they are privatized, as they tend to exist within the public sector. At the same time, social democratic and indeed other parties are facing the general neoliberal attack that demands demolition of public services in favour of cutting taxes and enabling more private spending. Social democrats (and others) have been quick to see a compromise here: if private firms can make soft profits out of providing public services, this might lessen the ideological attack on public spending. The system that results, whereby governments continue to pay for services and become the 'customers' but corporations produce them on a monopoly basis, reducing citizens to mere 'users', looks like becoming the central social pact of the early twenty-first century, at least in those societies that retain much in the way of public services at all. As Jonathan Tritter has argued, it is significant that this form of outsourcing has been particularly prominent in the Nordic countries, the world's leaders in the provision of public services. The resulting pattern of powerful corporations, relatively weak governments and passive citizens corresponds to the emerging pattern of power relations in neoliberal societies. It preserves basic features of the welfare state; and it provides monopoly profits to those firms who devote resources to cultivating relations with public officials. But it connives at an unhealthy intertwining of political and economic power, which in turn contributes to the growing inequality in power and wealth that is another major and disturbing hallmark of our societies. This is a Faustian social pact, the price of which is the soul of the welfare state.

Presenting alternatives to this vision is not difficult. The problems lie in wielding the power resources necessary to realize them. Indeed, the dominance of neoliberalism has not been the uninterrupted triumphal progress that it is sometimes represented as being. At the beginning of the present century some of the important institutions that had taken neoliberal positions on a number of central issues had started to revise their views. In 2002 the Nobel-Prize-winning former chief economist of the World Bank, Joseph Stiglitz, articulated a major critique of the Bank's application of free-market principles in developing countries. Ten years later (in 2012) he launched a similar attack on the damage being done to the world economy by rising inequality. Although Stiglitz had been required to leave the World Bank's employment because of his views, the Bank itself began to resile from its earlier stance. It began to be concerned at the neglect of public infrastructure and social needs that free-market doctrine involved, and at the growing inequalities it seemed to provoke.

The IMF and World Bank also began slightly to revise the ways in which they ranked countries in their annual *Doing Business* report. This had allocated points to countries according to the extent to which they maintained neoliberal (i.e., unregulated market) policies, including on the labour market. The countries that achieved the highest rankings were those that had no trade unions, no minimum wages, no protection against unfair dismissal, no compensation for unemployment. The International Labour Office (ILO), another, older international organization set up, like the Bank and IMF, to achieve some order in the international economy, pointed out repeatedly that this meant that only countries that defied ILO conventions could achieve the highest marks for 'doing business' in terms of labour policies. By 2009 The Bank and IMF had accepted the force of some of the ILO's arguments and had removed the labour section from the indicators used to rank countries in its *Doing Business* reports. The labour section continues as a separate part of the report, but now includes some limited information on whether countries maintain minimum standards. At the same time, as the International Trades Union Congress (ITUC) has pointed out, both the Bank and the IMF continue to issue national reports that praise countries that have followed the original strategy of removing workers' protection and rights to union representation.

The Organization for Economic Co-operation and Development (OECD), which in the 1990s had baldly advocated the unprotected exposure of workers to labour-market competition, had by 2006 also begun to speak of the need for improving labour skills and of finding ways of reconciling workers' needs for security with the market's need for flexibility. By 2011 it too, like Stiglitz, had started to express concern at the growing inequalities generated by prevailing economic policies. Meanwhile, the European Union, which had maintained an uneasy balance between a general commitment to neoliberal economic policies with some regard for a so-called 'social Europe', seemed to have found a more constructive compromise in the idea of 'flexicurity', drawn initially from Danish and Dutch labour and social policies, and discussed in the academic public policy literature by such scholars as Ruud Muffels and Ton Wilthagen. In place of the all-out attack on all kinds of labour protection, this approach distinguished between those policies that seemed just to protect a minority of workers in their present jobs, making innovation and change difficult for employers, and those that enabled workers to cope with change in an environment of trust and security. Included in the former would be rights to enable workers to avoid dismissal; among the latter would be high levels of unemployment pay and assistance in job searches and retraining. This is a theme to which we shall return at several points, as it provides an example of the difference between defensive and assertive social democracy. At the time of writing, however, the European story has not continued on this promising track. First, attempting to generalize the idea of 'flexicurity' so that almost every member state could claim to be practising it, the EU allowed its definition to become so general as to be almost meaningless. For example, central to the Danish model is the role of strong trade unions which, together with some other labour-market characteristics, enable workers to feel trust in the ability and willingness of the institutions to help them look after their interests. Without that trust basis, it is doubtful if formal structures could achieve their ends. This factor has not featured in official EU flexicurity policy.

Far worse was to follow. Greece had to apply to the EU, the European Central Bank (ECB) and the IMF (the so-called 'Troika') for massive support to protect it from a public debt crisis that was itself a consequence of the 2008 global crisis of private finance. The terms of its deal (as set out in the Memorandum of Understanding of February 2012) marked a return to the simple-minded neoliberalism of the 1990s. The country was to dismantle most labour-market regulation and protection, and reduce the role of collective bargaining (and therefore of trade unions) in setting minimum wages and to reduce labour-market protection. The main aims of the labour-market sections of the conditions were to expose workers to the full force of global labour-market competition, requiring the country to compete on low prices alone; forget about up-skilling and improving the quality of the labour force. The only interest shown by the Troika in infrastructural issues such as transport and energy was to ensure their privatization and therefore profit-making opportunities for other European corporations, as though that was all that would be needed to ensure an up-grading of facilities. The document showed no substantive interest in upgrading as such.

The same approach was also applied to other countries in difficulties: Ireland, Italy, Portugal and Spain. Outside the Eurozone, the British applied it to themselves. Come the crisis, EU, ECB and IMF and many national policy-makers have treated all sophisticated discussion of how to achieve competitiveness through upgrading as so much baggage, and have turned back to crude, unreconstructed neoliberalism. A crisis caused by appalling greed and irresponsibility among the world's leading private-sector banks was redefined as a crisis of public finances, and taxpayers were required to come to the bankers' aid.

True, the terms of the Greek bail-out include some valuable reforms to require the efficient functioning of public institutions – a really important issue in that country. There are also items that are unwelcome to the country's wealthy elite, such as major drives against tax evasion, corruption and making excessive profits in the provision of pharmaceuticals. Further requirements for the reform of how the main professions conduct their business match both neoliberal and social-democratic agendas. But the main burden of a cost-reduction strategy falls on ordinary working people, particularly public employees, who are among the relatively few who cannot engage in tax evasion. Their wage cuts and redundancies are certain to occur, because easily guaranteed. Whether the rich and Greece's exceptionally large numbers of self-employed will pay full taxes, and whether corruption will be rooted out and major efficiency gains made in public services must be more doubtful. Given that Greece has to continue to buy raw materials and semi-finished goods on world markets, it is only labour and social policy costs that can be reduced to achieve price competitiveness. For Greek workers the path to an assertive social democracy – which requires public investment in labour and many other factors of production – has been cut off. They are reduced either to fighting defensive battles to protect rights that in themselves will achieve little that is oriented to the future, or to accepting years of austerity until their labour costs can compete with those of Eastern Europe or the Far East. It is doubtful if the country's elite will share much of this fate with them. Based mainly on shipping activities and keeping its wealth in safe, untaxable havens, this elite is 'off-shore' in both literal and metaphorical senses.

At least in part, the 'Troika' has been responding to a perceived need to satisfy 'the markets', which means a need to please what are felt to be the demands and prejudices of traders in the global money and stock markets. They are not interested in whether presently unsuccessful countries can improve their performance by creating better infrastructures, or in what ways the balance between security and flexibility in the labour market can be reorganized to provide better lives for workers and more efficient economies. They are interested only in short-term gain from trading; while their preference as very wealthy individuals is for regimes of low taxation and of minimal rights for people at the foot of the economic hierarchy.

Greece is an extreme case among EU nations, but extreme cases often tell us something more general, as we can extrapolate from the characteristics that more of us share. Greece is extreme, but not atypical, in having an elite that, while exercising considerable control over the country (through its funding of parties and ownership of mass media), has become global and made its own fortunes more or less independent of the country itself. Greece is not untypical in having a working population faced with a choice between defending certain past social policy achievements that have ceased to have future utility, and giving these up in exchange for nothing other than full exposure to the insecurity of market forces. We can feel that our situation might be somewhat better than that of the Greeks only if we are confident that we can subject the power of the wealthy to some regulation, and find some means of developing future-oriented rather than defensive social policy. It is increasingly difficult to feel that confidence, since everywhere, not only in Greece, the priority of public policy has become guaranteeing the financial health of banks (albeit with them being required to abide by some conditions), leaving the rest of us to face the rigours of a neoliberalism that is being imposed, not so much because policy-makers believe in them so much anymore, but because they save money for that greater priority. Aditya Chakrabortty (*Guardian*, 2 April 2012) has drawn attention to the fact that the International Institute for Finance, a lobby group representing 450 private banks across the world, was an active participant in the discussions of the Troika over setting the terms of bank involvement in resolving the Greek crisis, a privilege not extended to any members of Greek civil society.

The present situation is therefore confused. Authoritative bodies are beginning to see the limitations of unmediated neoliberalism, but the powerful private actors in the financial markets to whom public policy must pander are entirely unconcerned at this. The problem for social democratic policies is not, as is often claimed, a paucity of ideas, but a paucity of power. However, the revising of views that has been taking place among major international organizations shows that there are at least potential openings in the neoliberal wall.

Rediscovering Social Democracy

What remains to be done at the level of ideas is not just to lay bare the internal contradictions of neoliberalism, but to demonstrate that some of its own stated objectives could in fact be better achieved through an adaptation of social democracy. This then becomes a means of redefining social democracy for the years ahead. Such an approach does not dispose of the problem of power imbalance. But popular discontent with some of the outcomes of actually existing neoliberalism may soon create conditions in which dominant elites are required to face the possibility of compromise.

A problem with such a proposed agenda, of social democracy reinterpreted in terms of neoliberalism, is that it seems to retrace the steps of the Third Way and the *Neue Mitte* criticized above. It must be acknowledged that these movements made a major contribution by drawing attention to the impossibility and indeed undesirability of the old socialist project of trying to transcend capitalism. Their error was to go beyond accepting capitalism and to accept it uncritically – in particular not seeing any problem in the accumulation of corporate power, especially in the global economy. A reformulation of social democracy needs to understand that this ended by creating more problems than it solved.

Plan of the Book

Explication of the meaning of this last ambiguous sentence is the theme of the next chapter. This will bring us to three kinds of neoliberalism, towards which, it is suggested, social democracy should have varied relationships.

The heart of the neoliberal project is the process of marketization, which leads in turn to consideration of whether this process satisfies all that we need from public life, and how assertive social democracy should relate to both marketization and its inadequacies. This is the topic of Chapter 3.

Particularly important for dealing with market inequalities are social policies, the welfare state. Chapter 4 discusses how recently developed ideas of a 'social investment welfare state' play a major part in shifting from defensive to assertive social democracy. It is important here not to lapse into purely technical discussions of policy, and to remember that social policy is always at the heart of conflict among different class interests.

Chapter 5 then considers the relationship between different balances of class power, different forms of the welfare state, and the association between these and economic success. This discussion is based on evidence from social science research. In order to avoid cluttering the text with statistics and graphs, details of the evidence are included in an Appendix to Chapter 5, to be found at the end of that chapter. The threats facing the social investment welfare state project are discussed in Chapter 6, where particular attention is paid to the roles of the EU and the USA.

Earlier chapters argued that social democracy does have some affinity with certain interpretations of neoliberalism, or at least of liberalism. This is pursued in more detail in Chapter 7, which sees important potential in the challenges that social democracy poses as the main source of diversity in an increasingly claustrophobic neoliberal orthodoxy. This opens the way to social democracy claiming to be the friend of innovation and novelty – a long way from its predominant defensive version. Chapter 8 turns to some key actors who have been neglected for much of the book: the social democratic, socialist and labour parties. What can we expect from them in constructing an assertive social democracy? Finally, Chapter 9 maps out some of the elements of a practical political agenda that might flow from the book's arguments.

References

Crouch, C. 2003. *Post-Democracy*. Cambridge: Polity.

Crouch, C. 2011. *The Strange Non-Death of Neoliberalism*. Cambridge: Polity.

European Commission 2007. *Towards Common Principles of Flexicurity*. Luxembourg: Office for Official Publications of the European Communities.

Government of Greece 2012. Memorandum of Understanding on Specific Economic Policy Conditionality, 9 February 2012. Athens: Government of Greece.

OECD 1994. *The Jobs Study*. Paris: OECD.

OECD 2006. *Boosting Jobs and Incomes. Policy Lessons from Reassessing the OECD Jobs Strategy*. Paris: OECD.

OECD 2011. *Divided We Stand: Why Inequality Keeps Rising*. Paris: OECD.

ILO 2007. *The Doing Business Indicators: Measurement Issues and Political Implications*. Economic and Labour Market Paper 2007/6. Geneva: ILO.

ITUC 2008. *The IFIs' Use of* Doing Business *to Eliminate Workers' Protection*. Washington DC: ITUC.

Muffels, R. (ed.) 2008. *Flexibility and Employment Security in Europe: Labour Markets in Transition*. Cheltenham: Edward Elgar.

Philips, K. and Eamets, R. 2007. *Approaches to Flexicurity: EU Models*. Luxembourg: Office for Official Publications of the European Communities.

Stiglitz, J. 2002. *Globalization and its Discontents*. London: W. W. Norton.

Stiglitz, J. 2012. *The Price of Inequality*. London: Allen Lane.

Tritter, J. 2011. 'Trouble in Paradise: The Erosion of the Nordic Welfare State', unpublished paper, conference on 'Beyond the Public Realm?' Coventry: University of Warwick Business School.

Wilks, S. 2013. *The Political Power of the Business Corporation*. Cheltenham: Edward Elgar.

Wilthagen. T. and Tros, F. 2004. 'The Concept of "Flexicurity": A New Approach to Regulating Employment in the Labour Market'. Transfer, 10, 2: 166–86.

World Bank. Annual. Doing Business. http://www.doingbusiness.com

World Bank 2011. *Report of the Employing Workers Methodology Consultative Group*. Washington, DC: World Bank.

2

We Are All (Partly) Neoliberals Now

In 1887 The British Liberal politician Sir William Harcourt declared in the House of Commons 'We are all socialists now' (*Hansard*, 11 August 1887). Although a preposterous over-statement, it represented recognition by many Conservative and Liberal politicians that the state would in future have to play a greater part in securing the welfare and security of the mass of the population, and in developing the infrastructure of a modern economy and society. There is a sense in which a discussion of overall socio-economic political strategy today must start with a similarly restricted recognition that 'We are all neoliberals now'.

To grasp what this implies, we need to distinguish among three different meanings of the idea of neoliberal:

- First are the pure neoliberals, who believe that society will be at its best when the conditions of perfect markets can be achieved in all areas of life, with extensive competition among multiple producers and with the role of the state restricted to maintaining the conditions necessary for such markets to operate. That does not imply a weak state; it is strong in protecting property rights, extending the role of markets to ever further areas and guaranteeing competition. But it limits itself to these tasks. I term this 'neoliberalism of the first kind'.

- Second are those who, while accepting the value and priority of markets in the economy, are aware of their limitations and deficiencies, in particular their inability to cope with externalities and public goods. They also believe that the market is not appropriate in some areas of life and wish to protect these from it. They differ from socialists in that they accept the superiority of a capitalist economy over a state-owned one, but do seek to use the state and other non-market institutions to remedy what they perceive as the market's defects. Various combinations of social democrats, environmentalists, religious groups, conservatives and others are found within this critical 'neoliberalism of the second kind'.

- Third is what we might call 'actually existing' neoliberalism, which refers to the amalgam of corporate lobbying of governments and the deployment of corporate and other private wealth in politics that today usually accompanies introduction of the neoliberal agenda. This is 'neoliberalism of the third kind'. Aspects of this were attacked in the previous chapter. It produces a politicized economy very remote from what economists understand by a liberal market economy, and a polity so unbalanced by plutocratic power that it seriously compromises the idea of liberal democracy. Like actually existing socialism in the old Soviet bloc, actually existing neoliberalism stands diametrically opposite to its originating idea at many points.

We need to consider these three kinds of neoliberalism in more detail. The most succinct statement of what I mean by the second, critical kind is to be found in the 1959 Bad Godesberg programme of the German Social Democratic Party (SPD): *Wettbewerb soweit wie möglich. Planung soweit wie nötig!* (Competition as far as possible. Planning as far as necessary!) This was later generalized by Karl Schiller, finance minister in Willy Brandt's government, to read *So viel Markt wie möglich; so viel Staat wie nötig* (as much market as possible, as much state as necessary). German Social Democracy in that period might seem an odd place and time to find a major enunciation of the core neoliberal principle, but in fact the geopolitical logic was clear. The West German SPD needed to separate itself absolutely from the monster of 'actually existing socialism' that was showing its appalling attributes the other side of the barbed wire in East Germany, the so-called German Democratic Republic. The state socialist system clearly prioritized the state as the source of all initiative and control, in both the private lives of its citizens and the conduct of the economy. At that time it did not have the reputation for inefficiency that it was later to acquire; the Soviet Union was about to succeed in putting a man into space, in advance of the USA, and the gap in living standards between east and west Germans was not yet so wide. But in 1953 a workers' protest in East Berlin had been put down by tanks and slaughter by occupying Russian forces – the incident that led even Bertolt Brecht, an East German public hero, to wonder ironically whether the government should not 'dissolve the people and elect another' (*löste das Volk auf und wählte ein anderes*). The SPD was distinguishing itself from the socialist regime in East Germany largely on grounds of human freedom. It was for this reason that it believed in giving priority to free choices within the market, bringing in the state only when 'necessary'. Today we have additional grounds for preferring markets as efficient allocators of resources, enabling citizens to engage in masses of transactions and choices without a need to keep referring to a central authority. A major advantage of a market economy is the scope it provides for choice among alternatives, rapid change and adaptation, and the encouragement of innovation; attributes that were not so obvious in the 1950s. And choice does not just provide something for consumers at the point of purchase; it gives providers an incentive to ensure that the quality of their goods and services is high, so that in a free market they will continue to be chosen. Therefore, 'the market where possible' has even more force today than in the 1950s.

But still, 'the state where necessary'. The formula is neat, but begs the big question: when and why does the state become necessary? Developments in regulatory economics enable us to provide four general reasons why we might be dissatisfied with the outcomes of free markets, and want to call on the state – or perhaps some other institution – to come to our aid. These are imperfect competition, inadequate information, the existence of public goods and the existence of negative externalities.

Market Inadequacies

These problems with markets are usually termed market 'failures'. I shall here use instead the notion of market 'inadequacies', which includes the idea of market failure but goes further. The narrower term implies that, provided it can be fixed in a particular case, the market is perfectly able to cope with the task in hand. There are however many instances where markets are simply unable to help us; they are just inadequate. This will become particularly important in Chapter 3, where we shall explore major problems in the development of market societies. Here we first concentrate on instances at a more micro level.

Imperfect competition

The first, imperfect competition, refers to a potential gulf between the theoretical requirements of free markets and actually existing markets. For markets to work the way that economists say they will, there must be many producers and many consumers; no one producer or consumer should be in a position to influence the market price by his/her/its actions alone, and they must not conspire together to do so; it must be easy for producers and consumers both to leave and enter the market. It can be shown that, if these conditions are absent, markets do not do their work of bringing producers and consumers together in ways that enable both to exercise choice while achieving overall efficiency. Real markets often do lack one or more of these conditions. It might be practically impossible to have more than a small number of producers serving particular consumers, as with many public utilities. In real markets it may be difficult for new firms to enter, because of high start-up costs, or to leave (remember the banks that were defined in 2008 as being 'too big to fail', i.e. to leave the market). Some firms may be sufficiently large within a market to be able to manipulate prices – even without resorting to the criminal behaviour of the kind that a number of global, ostensibly respectable British and other banks practised on the London Inter-Bank Lending Rate from around 2005 until 2012. In some of these cases markets might be able to correct themselves, but in others the defect will only worsen – that is, if enough powerful actors benefit from it and can keep it from public gaze. The 'state where necessary' may therefore be called upon to act, whether by ensuring that markets are working properly (e.g. by breaking up monopolies), by regulating their operation so that the power of dominant firms is not abused or by removing a sector from the market altogether if it appears that markets simply cannot be made to work satisfactorily within it.

It should be noted that identifying these problems of markets in no way denies the validity of a market economy; indeed, this critique assumes a preference for true markets, and is therefore fully compatible with economic theory and with neoliberalism – with reservations to be discussed below. Social democrats have indeed often been found insisting on a need for more competition more insistently than the conservative political forces that often espouse the free market more emphatically in their rhetoric. For example, Martin Höpner has shown how governments headed by the SPD have imposed more competition rules on German banks than have those headed by Christian Democrats. The most explicit state document in recent British history that advocated the strengthening of market forces in order to combat market failure was produced by a Labour government and co-authored by the then Chancellor of the Exchequer and later Prime Minister Gordon Brown. In the USA, Democratic administrations and agencies have been associated with a stronger prosecution of competition law than Republicans – to the extent that some neoliberal critics, such as the leading anti-trust judge Robert Bork, have labelled pro-market anti-trust law as communist.

Inadequate information

The second area of market inadequacy, the problem of inadequate information, is also concerned with the efficient functioning of markets and does not question *ab initio* their suitability. It is through his work on this problem that Joseph Stiglitz won his Nobel Prize; the problem is not a minor one. Economic theory assumes that market participants have perfect information – or at least as much information as they need – in order to make optimal decisions about the price, quality and other attributes of goods and services that they are buying and selling. It further assumes that rational actors would ensure that they did this, and therefore that, if we seem sometimes not to take much care in acquiring information before making a choice, then we had taken a prior decision that the choice was not sufficiently important to merit spending much effort or money on doing so. We can illustrate this argument by considering customers choosing between two brands of toothpaste, where they might reasonably assume that the various brands are much of a muchness and make a random choice. A very different case is presented by the investment bankers, who, in the run-up to the 2008 crisis, did not bother to seek information about the content of the bundles of assets that they were trading. The fact that a proportion of these assets were at best worthless turned out to be a major factor in provoking the crisis. According to the theory, these highly rational actors, with all technical means of calculating asset values available to them, should have been so motivated that they would never make an unwise market choice. In reality, the speed with which they were needing to make transactions, combined with the fact that they were interested only in prices in secondary markets and not the asset values indicated in primary ones, favoured a short-term rationality of ignoring information. More accurately perhaps, one should say that they had shifted their attention to a secondary and more easily attainable form of information: the set of beliefs about the set of beliefs (etc., etc.) that they perceived to be believed by others trading in the same markets. This was an entirely self-referential form of information. Such beliefs remain self-sustaining until – as will inevitably happen – someone significant starts to have doubts. Then the whole edifice collapses, as it did in 2008. It then gives way to a situation in which investors believe that other investors believe (etc., etc.) that there is a general belief that things will continue to be bad. In that situation banks become highly reluctant to lend any money at all. That is the situation in which we are now living. Central banks, governments and firms needing loans for investment can take whatever initiatives they like; they will find it very hard to change financial operators' new investment behaviour, because the only information they consider is each other's beliefs, not anything that is going on in the 'real' economy or public policy. The fact that, as a result of their initial excessively risky behaviour, the banks produced a crisis from which governments rescued them with guarantees from tax-payers' money, turned this information failure into one that indicated 'the state where necessary'.

More everyday examples of where information problems suggest a case for public intervention concern choices confronting ordinary citizens, who do not have the means to acquire the information they would need to make a wise choice over matters more substantial than choice of tooth-paste. For example, can children or their parents be expected to know the value of education to them in twenty or thirty years' time? One expects a negative answer to this question; hence publicly provided and funded education, together with ongoing conflict about the age after which one might start to expect positive answers and therefore children (or their parents) to make and/or fund educational choices. Similar arguments apply to decisions whether we ought to insure ourselves against illness, disability, unemployment, old age and other risks that might prevent us from earning a living. These have typically also become areas of public policy and funding, though to a varying extent in different societies, indicating that this too is an area of conflict. There are also many products that we buy in everyday markets, particularly technically complex ones, where it may be extremely difficult for consumers to access adequate information. Where the risks consequent on erroneous purchases and the temptations for producers to give misleading information are both high, there is often (though by no means always) government intervention and the establishment of legally binding obligations on producers: the small print in insurance policies, the labelling of food ingredients, electrical safety. In many other cases – for example the quality of vacuum cleaners, or computer equipment and software – we are left to make do as best we can, with the help of various commercial or civil-society agencies set up to advise consumers on such choices. Again, there is diversity across societies and change over time, indicating a contested boundary. Intervention might take the form of helping markets to operate more efficiently (for example, by improving information flows, as with ingredient labelling); or of regulating markets (as with the electrical safety standards of products permitted to be offered for sale); or of removing products from market provision altogether (as with many forms of education, social insurance and health care).

Public goods

The two final categories of market inadequacy (the existence of public goods and the existence of negative externalities) are more hotly contested. Public goods are defined tightly by economists to refer to goods (in the widest definition of that term as things that are highly desired) that are 'non-rival and non-excludable'. The first term, 'non-rival' means that the consumption by one person of a good does not prevent another person consuming it too. If you and I both possess radio sets, we can both access radio waves without diminishing the other's access to them. Radio waves are a public good. The same is not true of a glass of wine; if I am drinking it, you cannot do so as well. Access to radio waves cannot therefore be marketed, as they do not possess that quality that a good needs in order for a price to be set for it: scarcity. This holds unless some means can be found of preventing people from having access to radio waves without paying for them. Hence the second criterion for a public good: non-excludability. If it is impossible to exclude people from the enjoyment of a non-rival good, then it cannot be provided in the market.

In a pure market economy, goods that cannot be provided by the market will not be provided at all; things that have the quality of public goods will therefore not exist. If they are there already, as in the case of features in the natural environment, they are likely to be damaged or neglected, as no one has a market incentive to care for them. If no one could make money from radio waves, then in the normal course of events, no radio programmes would be made or broadcast. This is what economists call 'the tragedy of the commons', the tendency for things that are not in private ownership in a market context to become the responsibility of no one and to suffer from neglect. As with imperfect competition and information failure, there are three possible responses to this problem of public goods. First, one can argue that the good concerned is unimportant and allow the neglect to take place. Second, one can try to turn it into a marketable good. In the case of radio waves, it was possible for public authorities to control access among potential broadcasters, if not listeners. Access to specified wave lengths could therefore be sold to broadcasters, who could then charge firms and others who wanted to advertise their goods on the wave length. This makes a market, not out of the relationship between broadcasters and listeners, but between broadcasters and advertisers. Listeners are not customers, just users; the broadcasters have an indirect interest in pleasing them to the extent that, if people do not listen to a station, no one will have an interest in advertising on it. A third solution is for government to establish a public agency with responsibility for caring for the public good (in our example, a public body to provide radio programmes, funded by general taxation or – if feasible – a special tax levied from the owners of radio sets), without making use of private ownership.

Externalities

Finally, externalities are by-products of market activity, which do not form part of the costs of that activity. They can be positive, as with the pleasant aromas around a baker's shop; the baker cannot charge passers-by from sniffing the aromas, even though they result from his/her activities – though of course some passers-by might be lured by them to come into the shop to buy bread and cakes. But it is negative externalities that are the centre of interest of public policy. The most obvious examples are pollution – as, for example, when chemicals released from factory chimneys damage the health of large numbers of persons in the vicinity. Again there are three potential approaches. First, one can argue that an externality is insufficiently important to warrant public attention – more exactly, that if those damaged by the externality do not find it worthwhile to pay the firm to abate the nuisance, then the damage done to them is not as great as the loss that would occur to the firm if it was forced to cease the activity. Second, taxes or other charges might be devised to make polluters pay, to the extent that they will find it cheaper to change their production processes than to pay the charges. This is a market solution, in that it works on the cost incentives facing firms, though government action is required to impose the taxing or charging regime. Third, regulations can be devised and imposed that make pollution a criminal act.

Conflicts within Neoliberalism

Within an overall neoliberal economy, there can be debate and conflict over how to tackle issues of market inadequacy. What was described above as neoliberalism of the first kind refers to an approach to these issues that: (1) takes it for granted that there will be general gains from easing restrictions on market forces; (2) predominantly takes up the first of the three possible remedial positions that we have identified in each case, that is, arguing that a posited market inadequacy is trivial or unimportant; (3) but, once having accepted the importance of an inadequacy, opts for the approach to tackling it that involves making the market work better rather than using some form of public intervention instead of the market (the second options discussed in each of our cases).

The terms of the EU, ECB and IMF bail-out conditions for Greece discussed in Chapter 1 represent an example of neoliberal thinking of this first kind. In the interests of improving the 'business-friendly' environment of Greece, it requires the drastic reduction of various regulations in certain sectors of the economy, specifically including health and safety and the food industry as examples of cases where this is needed. Presumably it should be left to the market to discover the limits to consumers' taste for unsafe, unhealthy food products. The conditions also require the easing of planning controls on building projects, while at the same time advocating strengthening of the country's important tourist industry. It would not occur to a neoliberal economist that much of Greece's tourism depends precisely on the maintenance of certain restraints on modern building activities.

Similarly, the bail-out conditions require a liberalization of the rules governing the professions and some other regulated trades. Rules governing professions comprise a difficult mix of two factors, which become deeply intertwined and can be separated only with great skill and care: on the one hand, regulations necessary to safeguard standards; on the other, rules for limiting access to an occupation in order to strengthen the market position of its practitioners. The problem is that practitioners have a strong incentive to use the former to achieve the latter, and that constitutes the case for a neoliberal bias in favour of deregulation. There are, however, important babies in the bathwater of professional regulation. A simple attack on all regulation runs the risk of demolishing safeguards of standards on which consumers depend, especially in areas (like law and medicine) where specialized knowledge is required in order to make sound judgements in the free market. All this is ignored in the Greek bail-out terms, which require deregulation with no mention of those aspects of regulation that might be needed to protect consumers. Throughout the competitiveness sections of the document only one simple remedy is offered: more market.

The Greek bail-out terms are an easy target, for they present a rare case of a fully explicit specification of the neoliberal agenda imposed by *Diktat* on a whole country; but examples can be found in any country and from a multitude of neoliberal sources. Another major instance was the dismantling of industries in East Germany following the collapse of the state socialist regime in 1990. An institution, the *Treuhand*, was established to oversee the break-up of assets and their sale at reduced prices to west German corporations. The *Treuhand* had a neoliberal mandate and acted on the taken-for-granted assumption that everything in the east was of poor quality and operated at low standards of efficiency. Businesses were sold very cheaply to west German firms, with the great majority of workers being made redundant. In the majority of cases this may have been the only solution, but there were important exceptions. The neoliberal dogmatism of the *Treuhand* did not permit it to consider such a possibility, and some valuable assets, such as the famous Zeiss optical works at Jena and elsewhere were sold off far too cheaply and excessively reduced.

If neoliberals of the first kind have an ongoing bias in favour of market solutions and of ignoring issues that will not respond to this medicine alone, those of the second kind see a wider diversity of potential approaches to problems. Social democrats, environmentalists, various kinds of conservatives and others are keen – sometimes too keen – to identify market inadequacies, proposing that they are serious enough to warrant intervention, and (possibly though not necessarily) preferring market-transcending to market-improving approaches. Many, perhaps most, political struggles in democratic countries can be interpreted in terms of these confrontations. However, the positions that particular movements or individuals adopt will not necessarily always be predictable. As already noted, the German SPD has been eager to increase banking competition. US conservative Republicans, who normally take up fairly extreme neoliberal positions, are strongly opposed to the abortion of pregnancies, even if abortions are carried out in private clinics, and demand state action to ban abortion. Feminist movements, normally hostile to many neoliberal political positions, usually seek the entry of women into the paid labour force, which represents the marketization of women's work, once 'protected' from the market by the family and household. But in general, over the main range of political issues of the day, neoliberals should be expected to take up market-intensifying positions, and social democrats and others to be more sceptical and to favour transcending markets through government action and regulation.

An important middle ground is constituted by those approaches, usually requiring government action, that seek to restructure markets so that they give appropriate incentives to market participants. Perhaps the main evidence that the overall consensus had shifted further in a neoliberal direction than anticipated by the SPD's 1959 formula has been the acceptance by many social democrats, in particular when in government, that such approaches may constitute a perfectly satisfactory approach, sometimes indeed superior to the use of more direct government intervention. This can be seen in the growing preference for 'polluter pays' approaches over direct regulatory control to dealing with environmental damage. A good example, which illustrates several of the themes of this book, is the EU's carbon trading scheme (and similar schemes in other parts of the world).

Under a carbon trading scheme, firms in industries producing carbon emissions are given (or buy in an auction) permits to produce a certain level of polluting emissions during a particular period. If they exceed the permitted level they are fined. If they produce less pollution than permitted, they can sell the unused permits to firms unable or unwilling to make emissions reductions. Firms can also buy more permits if they fund emissions-reduction projects in developing countries to produce emission reductions equal to the increased emissions they have purchased (a process known as offsetting). This is a market solution in that it gives firms financial incentives to reduce pollution: incentives to be able to sell unused permits, negative incentives to avoid the cost of buying extra permits, incentives to participate in schemes for pollution reduction in developing countries. But it is not a 'pure' market approach, as the markets concerned are established by political authorities, and a system of sanctions has to be in place to ensure compliance. Doctrinaire neoliberals therefore oppose these schemes and have to resort to climate change denial instead; that is, deny that a public goods problem exists, because the pure market cannot cope with such problems.

The success of carbon trading schemes obviously depends on the initial level of emissions for which permits are sold being below the level of existing emissions. In setting this level authorities also have to bear in mind that some elements of the scheme provide sub-optimal incentives. If there is a surplus of unused permits, their price will be cheap, removing any incentive on firms buying them to contemplate pollution reduction instead. Offsetting might be used to finance projects that were going to take place anyway, and also removes pressure from firms in developed economies, by far the main sources of pollution around the world, to reduce their own emissions.

Evidence to date from the EU's scheme is that the authorities failed the initial test and have been issuing permits that allow far too high a level of emissions. This is partly because the global recession has produced unanticipated emissions reductions, but also because lobbies from leading polluting industries have been permitted to influence the setting of levels. The EU is always sensitive to arguments from business that too much legislation for social purposes will handicap European firms in competition with those from the USA and other parts of the world with lower standards. As a result of these two factors, there is a vast over-supply of emissions permits and therefore a fall in their price. This reduces all the benign incentives embodied in the scheme, and may even lead some firms in polluting industries to cancel plans for reducing their emissions, so cheap has it become to buy permits.

A further issue has been the development of secondary and derivatives markets in emissions permits. The majority of trades that take place in the carbon emissions markets are not between firms in the industries concerned, but between banks and hedge funds. They are generating exactly the kinds of complex secondary and derivatives markets that they produced in the financial system itself. Carbon permits are being bought and sold depending on what it is believed they can be bought and sold for within these markets, with decreasing reference to what is happening to carbon emissions themselves. There are two dangers here. First, this speculative market must eventually collapse, as do all speculative markets, producing another crisis of the kind we experienced in 2008. Second, just as many areas of public policy have been considerably distorted since 2008 as governments have decided they must compensate banks for their folly, so environmental policy and action to combat climate change will be diverted into measures to rescue the carbon trading market in order to rescue, not the planet, but banks and hedge funds.

Critics of the use of markets see these weaknesses as evidence that public policy should not make use of market forces, but should rely on direct controls or taxation. This is, for example, the stance of Friends of the Earth (FoE) in their report on carbon trading, *Dangerous Obsession*. But some of the defects FoE identify, such as evasion, occur with regulation and taxation too. If one of the problems with carbon trading is lack of will on the part of authorities, that same deficiency will weaken other approaches as well. The FoE critique certainly undermines the claim of many neoliberals that regulation is vulnerable to being undermined in a way that market forces are not. But the sad overall conclusion has to be that all approaches are vulnerable.

The two central lessons that emerge from the weakness of carbon trading scheme relate to themes that are central to this book. First, when corporate lobbies are able to bring economic power to bear within political decision-making – as accepted by neoliberals of the third kind, though not by those of the first and second kinds – the market economy is undermined. It is the role of corporate lobbies in ensuring soft targets in carbon trading schemes that have destroyed their effectiveness. Those who believe in the use of the market in public policy, whether they are diehard neoliberals of the first kind or social democrats willing to contemplate the use of markets when they can be effective, must grapple with this fundamental characteristic of contemporary capitalism before they can make any progress.

The second lesson is related but more specific. The tendency for unregulated financial institutions to produce dangerous speculative bubbles wherever a market exists is incompatible with the efficient functioning of the market economy itself and with attempts to pursue important public policy goals.

Does this mean that willingness to use market forces constitutes a 'sell-out' by social democrats, or the addition of a useful weapon to its armoury, particularly when government regulation itself has several failings, if only the problem of corporate and in particular banking power could be resolved? The key question is whether the proposed new strengthened markets themselves contain any inadequacies. We can illustrate this point by taking examples from each of our identified forms of market inadequacy.

First, on the question of imperfect competition, the pure neoliberal is likely to want to move to as fully competitive an economy as possible, extending competition to, for example, the privatization of public services. At a certain point here a social democrat will want to step back. Ignoring for the moment the important issue of whether it really is possible to get extensive competition in public service provision, the social democrat will be worried about distributional implications. Can a private market in, say, health or education, provide high quality services to all citizens, or do different markets develop for the rich and the poor, as with most private goods, like television sets or cars? If there are strong fears on these grounds, the social democrat is likely to prefer moving to a completely non-market form of provision, such as public service. Social democrats are also likely to worry that unrestrained competition will drive down labour standards, reducing wages and workers' ability to gain access to training and skill improvement. They may therefore support measures like organized collective bargaining between unions and employers' associations, to ensure certain guarantees and certainties for employees. The true neoliberal will not tolerate this at all, but will argue that labour conditions can be only as good as market competition allows. There is an important dilemma here for social democrats. If labour standards are deteriorating in the private sector at large as a result of intensified global competition, should social democrats try to protect islands of decent conditions in protected public services? Or does this create a gap between public-service labour-market insiders (protected by social democracy and trade unions) and the rest of the work force, which is left vulnerable and insecure? This is not an attractive strategy. It leaves a majority of the work force, not just outside the reach of the labour movement, but likely to become hostile to it.

A neoliberal who accepts the issue of market inadequacy in information provision might support legal regulation to ensure adequate dissemination of information to consumers, through labelling, the clear statement of contract terms and transparent pricing structures; but is more likely to prefer voluntary arrangements – provided these could not be seen as arrangements in restraint of trade. Social democrats are likely to worry that many consumers might not be able to make sense of the information provided by voluntary arrangements, and that the power of corporations will enable them to counter public information with expensive advertising. An example would be the attempt by firms producing unhealthy foods to associate themselves with images of sport and health, to offset the effect of information concerning the threats to health represented by certain ingredients. Social democrats are therefore more likely to want publicly funded education campaigns, not just lists of ingredients, to compete with corporate publicity; and regulation to *prevent*, not just warn against, the use of certain potentially harmful ingredients. Sometimes, as for example with private medical cures, where there is a risk that ill-informed consumers may waste their money on inappropriate treatments, they will want an area of activity to be removed entirely from the market and placed with public service professionals.

Neoliberals prefer to tackle public goods problems by making as many as possible of such goods private, as shown in the example of the licensing of commercial radio stations in order to ensure that the public good of air waves is developed. Such licensing might generate problems of imperfect competition if, because of high start-up costs, only a small number of firms is able to set up stations. Those pushing always for more neoliberal solutions are likely to tell us not to worry too much about that, provided we have solved the public goods problem. Social democrats are also likely to worry that, the number of wealth holders who can afford to buy major assets being small, such arrangements become devices for state guarantees of increased profits for large wealth holders, who also acquire from the state power over the disposal of public assets.

An interesting case that demonstrates many of these issues of public goods appeared in the UK in 2011 over plans by the Conservative–Liberal government to privatize the public forests – an asset held in state hands for public goods reasons. This followed the strict neoliberal preferences of many in both those parties: the state should not own resources that could be in private hands; private owners would have an incentive to maximize earnings from the forests, which would ensure efficiency in woodland maintenance and imaginative commercial policies for public access. There was however very considerable opposition, partly from social democrats opposing an asset passing into the private control of a few wealthy corporations and individuals, partly from environmentalists, but also from conservative rural interests not trusting that commercial incentives would encourage appropriate long-term forest management. The opposition proved so strong that the government withdrew the plans. Interestingly, this very diverse group of opponents preferred to continue to entrust the forests to a monopoly responsible to a government that wanted to privatize them rather than to owners in the private market. There was clearly a widespread belief that, in the case of an abuse of the forests, a public campaign would be generated more effectively through political channels than through the market.

Similarly with problems of externality, social democrats are likely to be suspicious of solutions like carbon trading, on the grounds that some offenders will use their freedom of choice to pay the cost of their pollution; this might bring useful revenue to public funds, but it would also leave a source of damage and harm in place. Neoliberals argue that this approach forgets that protecting the environment has a cost that needs to be placed in the equation against the cost of the damage. This argument is deployed, for example, to oppose government and local government schemes for recycling waste materials, such as glass, paper and used electric batteries. It is claimed that the cost of recycling is often higher than the cost of the materials recycled. This argument ignores the externalities and damage to public goods involved in the creation of landfill waste-disposal sites, which are often the only alternative to recycling.

In general, social democrats are also more likely than neoliberals to perceive an externality and to decide that something should be done about it. For example, to anticipate a major discussion of Chapter 4, the intensification of market forces intensifies insecurity in workers' lives. Their incomes and ability to remain in their jobs, their working conditions, all become liable to major uncertainty as demand and supply fluctuate. This insecurity produces a difficulty in managing personal life, leading to anxiety and sometimes even to distress. This is a by-product of the economic activity in question, but it does not enter into firms' cost calculations. It is an externality – unless such problems are limited to individual firms who do not manage their affairs efficiently, in which case workers will leave those firms for others who manage better, and there is no longer an externality. If the cause of the insecurity is exogenous and affects a whole sector or the overall economy, then there is real externality. Neoliberals are reluctant to accept that anything can be done about such problems without weakening firms' ability to cope with trade fluctuations. They might accept some minimal level of unemployment compensation combined with strong negative incentives to persuade workers who lose their jobs to accept whatever work is available, however badly paid and in however poor conditions. Social democrats are likely to see a need for a whole raft of measures: unemployment pay, redundancy compensation, protection against dismissal, measures for retraining.

A clear pattern emerges from these discussions. While willing to examine market solutions to market inadequacies, social democrats always have at the back of their minds two anxieties:

- Since markets in a privately owned economy depend on property ownership, and since that ownership is extremely unequally divided, will market solutions strengthen the power imbalance between a small group of wealthy property owners and the rest of the population?

- Given that our ability to use markets depends on our income and wealth, markets will always produce inequalities in the distribution of goods and services that provide standards of living and life chances; how acceptable are these inequalities?

These concerns result from social democracy's core role as the political movement that represents the lower part of society's distribution of income and wealth. It is this, rather than a preference as such for the collective against the individual that ought to motivate its critique of markets. The frequent perception that the confrontation between social democracy and neoliberalism takes this latter form is the result of a misunderstanding, not so much of social democracy, but of the idea of the free market, a misunderstanding particularly widespread among neoliberals themselves. In all statements of the theory of the market, from the seventeenth century to contemporary textbooks, that institution is presented as a means whereby human action is coordinated in order to maximize universal gain. The market is supposed to ensure that, by using it, individuals can achieve their own goals only by maximizing a general interest. Market theory does not pit the individual against the collectivity, but tries to enable individuals to achieve their goals without harming the collectivity. Free-market theory and social democracy are alike in being oriented to collective interests. The latter appears more collectivist because it is more sceptical about the capacity of markets unaided to pursue those interests, particularly because of the difficulty of finding market solutions to public goods problems. But this scepticism should always be open to persuasion that in particular cases improving markets may well be the best solution to a problem.

The history of social democracy presents us with a fascinating paradox here. Until the modern period the working population, whether peasants or industrial workers, were seen as the 'private' classes. They played no part in the public institutions of court, state, municipality, urban guild that saw to the collective business of society. The idea survives today in the concept of the 'private' as the lowest rank in the army, the private soldier who lacks a 'public' commission. The person who is solely 'private' is someone who lacks something; they are 'deprived', in 'privation'. Aristocrats and, later, high bourgeois, took upon themselves responsibility (or, rather, claimed the honour and respect that would have been due had they accepted responsibility) for seeing to the common good. For the Conservative eighteenth-century English philosopher, Edmund Burke, the noble families of England present in the House of Lords preserved the constitution and the society by the very fact of their longevity. However, in reality it was only when the classes of the 'private', lower-class people began to make their presence felt on political regimes that the public realm as we know it really developed, with schools, sanitation, hospitals and many other public institutions. While eventually many political movements shared in campaigns for these goods, they have become the hallmark of social democracy. When seventeenth- and eighteenth-century aristocrats discovered what water engineers could achieve, they built fountains and artificial lakes on their private estates; they did not provide public supplies of drinkable water to the cholera- and typhoid-ridden populations of cities. It was the private classes of those whose interests were considered too narrow to risk granting them citizenship, and the political movements they generated, who became the custodians of collective goals. The paradox happened initially because workers' private resources were so small that they needed collective action where wealthier people could make private provision – for facilities as diverse as parks, medical care, education or security in old age. As choices between public and private provision started to become more feasible for larger proportions of the population as a result of the spread of markets, social democrats continued to remember those two distributional questions emphasized above.

Presented this way it would seem – and it is often claimed – that social democracy wants a market economy with one hand tied behind its back. Because of its anxieties about distributional issues, it is always that much more sceptical about market solutions, even where these would be the most efficient. Neoliberals, having no such inhibitions, will always go for the most efficient solution, which will eventually turn out to benefit everyone. The argument is enshrined in such sayings as 'better a smaller share of a large cake than a larger share of a small one', or 'a rising tide lifts all boats', and in the concept of 'trickle down'.

But this is to present a naive view of neoliberalism as the working out of some pure economic theories (which it rarely is) rather than as a political movement (which it really is). This brings us to examine in more detail the idea of neoliberalism of the third kind, the actually existing neoliberalism that is carried by political movements as much in need of support and constituencies as is social democracy. As we repeatedly note, many major markets are dominated by oligopolies and highly imperfect competition; in overall dominance is a financial system that has shown its dependence on, but ability to command, state support. As we saw in Chapter 1, such policies as the privatization of public services and public–private financing partnerships are very often a means whereby governments and oligopolies of private corporations do deals together – with ultimate consumers (whether small firms or individuals) having little say or chance to express their interests, whether through the market or through politics.

A frequent device, noted in Chapter 1, is for a separation in the role of 'consumer' between two separate figures of 'customer' and 'user'. Neoliberal political rhetoric does not recognize this difference, always conflating the two roles. They are separated, not only in public–private relations, but in many purely private-sector arrangements too. We have already met this in the case of private broadcasting, where the broadcaster's listeners are not its customers, that role being reserved to advertisers. A more specific broadcasting example can be taken from the sale of monopoly rights to televise sporting events. The market relationship is between the organization owning the event and the corporation buying the monopoly right. The firm buying the right is the only customer here. The people who watch the programmes are merely users, not customers. They have been customers at the point where they bought the right to buy the service, but that was simply the right to have it or not; since it is a monopoly, they cannot exercise the normal market right to choose among providers. One day the relationship between the sporting association and the broadcasting firm may break down, a different firm will buy the monopoly, and viewers will observe new logos, perhaps a change of presenters and presentation style. No one will have asked them whether they wanted a change or were dissatisfied with the previous style. They will have been completely passive in this process, with no more capacity to choose than citizens of Moscow during the Soviet period being told that they could choose to do their shopping in GUM.

This division of the role of consumer into active customer corporations and passive user individuals may seem considerably less important when it is a matter of watching football matches than when it is about receiving health care, but the point is to demonstrate how extensive are the twin phenomena of the power of corporations and the passivity of individual citizens in the neoliberal economy.

We can again use the conditions of the Greek bail-out to indicate the contradictions within neoliberal positions. The troika (EU, ECB, IMF) was very concerned to ensure the privatization of Greek transport and energy supplies. The only proposals it made to ensure improved quality in these sectors was privatization. But we know from experience in northern Europe that the privatization or contracting out of services that remain matters of public importance usually means the establishment of small oligarchies of politically favoured corporations. Complaints about the quality of services they offer and their pricing continue to be important political issues in France, Germany, the UK and the Nordic countries. Regulation remains essential to safeguarding consumer interests, and there are then problems around the capture of regulators by the service providers. Privatization does not bring consumer-sensitive supply or guarantee improved quality, just a different kind of politically privileged corporation. These newly privileged, unlike the old patriarchal firms of the Greek kind, speak the neoliberal jargon of transparency, corporate governance, consumer sovereignty, are on Facebook and Twitter, and sound very modern. But they are essentially playing the same game as the arrogant old patriarchs who knew nothing of such things: developing snug mutual relations with those who award contracts and regulate their conduct; hunting out markets where competition is very limited and where governments are involved and happy to become partners.

At first sight it is remarkable that a system of thought as simple-minded, dogmatic and corruptible as neoliberalism of the third kind should have escaped for so long with so little criticism. One has only to compare the intense and often bitterly unfair attacks launched by foundations with corporate funding and by mass media empires against the cautious and sophisticated work of the scientists who have been warning us about climate change. But there lies the answer: neoliberal remedies might ruffle the feathers of local oligarchies like the Greek elite, but only in order to open up markets to the large corporations of northern Europe and the USA, while climate-change scientists are criticizing the activities of precisely that kind of corporation. Once it engages in politics, neoliberal economics loses it innocence, and is not a neutral, technical force, but an ally of particular interests.

This kind of neoliberalism is the real political enemy of contemporary social democracy, as it subordinates general and widespread interests to those of a privileged few. Social democrats have conflicts, but manageable ones and legitimate debate with neoliberals of the first kind. But these latter are in danger of damaging many important causes that cannot be resolved through using the market. These include the familiar social democratic concerns of insecurity in the lives of working people and neglect of other collective interests and problems of other negative externalities. The most important of these issues are now a shared agenda of social democrats and environmental campaigners. Indeed, the more damage that neoliberalism does to life outside the market, the more it firms up the alliance between these two important forces.

References

European Commission 2009. *EU Emissions Trading Scheme.* Luxembourg: Office for Official Publications of the European Communities.

Friends of the Earth 2009. *A Dangerous Obsession: The Evidence Against Carbon Trading and for Real Solutions to Avoid a Climate Crunch.* London: FoE.

HM Treasury 2004. *Microeconomic Reform in Britain: Delivering Opportunities for All.* London: HMSO.

Höpner, M. 2004. *Sozialdemokratie, Gewerkschaften und organisierter Kapitalismus, 1880–2002.* MPIfG Discussion Paper 04/10. Cologne: Max Planck Institute for the Study of Societies.

3

Marketization and Market Inadequacies

Critics of neoliberalism increasingly rally round the figure of Karl Polanyi as an observer of the original growth of industrial capitalism whose arguments provided a basis for a critique of the new wave of its neoliberal, post-industrial form. He was part of that extraordinary generation of Jewish intellectuals who flourished in Vienna until the arrival of the Nazis sent them westwards. Polanyi went to the UK and the USA before settling in Canada, where in 1944 he wrote his *The Great Transformation*, a study of the growth of capitalism in England. He described how the introduction of the market during the spread of capitalism, first in agriculture and then in the industrial revolution, destroyed the fabric of social relationships of traditional society. This does not necessarily mean that one regrets the passing of all such relationships. Among those that were destroyed were the power of local landowners over the peasantry, at least some forms of the subordination of women, several aspects of the power of the church. The point is to note when a destruction occurs; to ask what the market puts in its place; to ask also whether this is an improvement; and, if not, to propose alternatives. The same questions arise for us now as at the end of the eighteenth century. We are in the midst of a major wave of marketization, this time uprooting not just some residual ancient practices, but the welfare state, ideas of employees' rights and other features of the social compromises that gave the second half of the twentieth century its distinctive character. What is being achieved, what damaged, by this process? These questions can be usefully considered by exploring briefly some of the main confrontations between markets and other institutions. This is in no sense an exhaustive discussion; the intention is to use examples to illustrate the dilemmas and complexities of both markets and attempts to address problems that they cause.

Marketization and Trust

We can begin with the case of trust. In traditional societies where modern markets have not penetrated, trading agreements are based on trust: I do a deal with you, either because on the basis of past experience I believe I can rely on you, or because I am confident that if you defect on the deal you will acquire a bad reputation in your community. This is a chancy business; means of enforcement are not well developed, and it is very difficult to move forward to doing the deals with strangers on which advanced economies depend. The market transforms this. One is able to do deals with another, possibly a complete stranger, provided one believes that the market itself is functioning. Provided one can believe that unreliable, incompetent or dishonest actors will be driven out of the market by the competitive process, and that if this fails there is an effective contract law (or adequate private means of dispute resolution), one needs neither belief in nor even knowledge about the personal probity or competence of the person with whom one is trading. The growth of the market therefore usually brings with it an increasingly sophisticated law of contract, which replaces trust between individuals with very precisely defined terms and definitions of how failure to perform will be dealt with, and clear understandings about how law might be used to resolve disputes. This is a considerable improvement over agreements based on trust alone, and is a major example of how the destruction by market forces of institutions typical of traditional societies amounts to a major advance.

But there are also losses. Contract law brings very high transaction costs, mainly involving the legal institutions needed for enforcement. More important to an account based on Polanyi's approach, the replacement of trust by contract can lead to the destruction of the institutions that had supported trust. Trust becomes unnecessary; therefore it is not cultivated and not valued; the mechanisms that supported it are neglected. People therefore find increasingly that they can no longer trust each other and have to rely more and more on contracts, the terms of which have to become ever more complex, ready to deal with ever more forms of dishonest behaviour. Trust becomes eroded even in areas of life outside the normal reach of the market, leading to the introduction of market and contract analogies to areas of life normally seen as beyond them. This, in turn, reduces the need for trust even further.

An important example that exhibits the deep ambiguity of this process is the growing tendency of patients to sue medical practitioners if treatments go wrong. Until a few decades ago patients were likely to trust their doctors, and to believe that they always did their best. They seem to be increasingly sceptical of this, and likely to believe that doctors are not trustworthy unless placed under the threat of likely legal action. The costs of medical provision are therefore increased by practitioners' needs to take out expensive insurance. When giving advice or proposing treatments to patients they need to think not only of the medical issues involved but also of likely legal implications, which may distort their medical judgement. There is then a growing tendency for lawyers to seek to expand the range of actionable issues in medical practice in order to expand their own role and earnings. These developments are at their most extreme in the USA, the advanced country in which the market enters most into medical practice and relationships, displacing one based purely on professional codes. Neither extreme position on this issue is attractive. 'Trust me, I'm a doctor' is not an acceptable prescription for that relationship; neither is one governed at every point by threats of, and elaborate protections against, recourse to the law courts. Once the excessive trust demanded by the traditional model is, legitimately, disturbed, how can we reach intermediate positions that balance trust against a more contractual relationship before we slip fully into the latter?

In a world where there is no need for trust and no cultivation of trust as a value, only 'mugs' behave in trustworthy ways; smart people sail as close as they can to the wind of contract law, seeing what they can get away with.

The contemporary financial system gives us further important examples of this phenomenon. National banking systems in, say, Germany or the UK, used to be dominated by rather small groups, who developed typical trust relations among each other based on family and friendship links. The London Stock Exchange had as its motto 'My word is my bond', the financial equivalent of 'Trust me, I'm a doctor.' Such arrangements are vulnerable to abuse – the confidence trickster preys precisely on such informality; they are restricted to small elites and difficult to penetrate; and there are severe limits on their capacity to grow. As Susanne Lütz has described in a study of what happened to the British and German systems during the global market liberalization process that began in the 1980s, these partly informal, network-based systems based on accumulations of local tradition came under attack, as they were not suited to the mass of rapid transactions among total strangers that constituted financial globalization. They were replaced by a more transparent, rule-based approach that enabled people to make financial transactions across the world with complete strangers. This required the establishment of new formal rules of contract. In practice and coincidentally this meant an Americanization of financial relationships; the USA as a relatively young country drawing its population from across the world had long had financial arrangements that did not depend on shared understandings among small groups. Hence the paradox that global financial liberalization meant the establishment of elaborate new legal systems of regulation, replacing informal arrangements.

One of many things revealed by the financial crisis of 2007 and 2008 was that in fact trust continued to play a role in relations among financial traders. When banks discovered that they had been selling each other bundles of bonds that contained what became known as 'toxic assets', they ceased lending to each other, leading to an increase in inter-bank lending rates that provoked a global liquidity crisis. The crisis has been interpreted as one of inadequate regulation, and this account is correct. But it was not only that; it was also a crisis of trust. It would seem that banks had not simply trusted that market mechanisms and contract law were enough to protect against malpractice; they had also trusted each other's professionalism in a rather old-fashioned way, and panicked when they realized that trust had been betrayed. In 2012 the extent of the betrayal was discovered to have gone even further, when it was learned that in London the main mechanism for fixing those rates at which banks lent to each other, the London Interbank Offered Rate (LIBOR), had been rigged by traders at several leading banks. These actions had broken UK criminal law, and later there were actions in US civil law. But in the chorus of criticism that greeted the revelations, there were also complaints of immorality as well as illegality. In other words, the bankers concerned were considered to have abused trust – implying that, despite all the prominent teachings of neoliberalism that the market alone could manage economic relationships, trust still plays an irreducible role in human interactions, even in this field of purest financial calculation.

This very important example can be seen as a contest between three sources of order, each of which failed: the old conservative institution of trust; the neoliberal institution of the market (aided by civil law); and the preferred social democratic preference of legal regulation. The thorough-going marketization of the financial sector had undermined both old trust-based arrangements and legal regulation.

Only the pure market remained, and it responded and started to correct itself only after enormous damage had been done. And participants in the system itself had clearly under-estimated the extent to which trust and regulation had been destroyed.

The lesson from this cautionary tale is that the market can destroy more than one realizes; and that one cannot rely on the market alone to provide equivalents for some functions that older, more implicit institutions were performing. Marketization had destroyed more of the basis of trust than it had replaced through the perfection of its calculations. The immediate lesson for societies experiencing the initial marketization that Polanyi described was of a need for public policy, including regulation, to run alongside, or immediately after, marketization to remedy, restore, if possible improve upon those arrangements that were being destroyed by its march. More generally, the only way to ensure that profit maximization does not conflict with trustworthiness is to have markets with such perfect transparency that no duplicity against ultimate consumers is possible. But that assumes more or less equal access to accurate information between corporations and consumers, and no asymmetrical capacity for corporations to produce information favourable to themselves and unfavourable to other interests. This could happen only if there were a reasonable equality of wealth and power in society. In a society where a small minority can maximize profit by taking advantage of the naive trust of the many, the appeal to remove regulation and rely on trust in personal responsibility alone is an appeal to permit exploitation to run forward unhindered.

Trust is a baby in the bathwater of traditional societies, at severe risk when the establishment of markets, followed rapidly by contract law, removes the plug. We want to lose the dirty water but keep the baby. This calls for careful design of marketization. We need neither the neoliberal extreme of pure marketization nor a socialist replacement of markets by state regulation, but arrangements that leave some role for trust in human exchanges – and therefore give us strong incentives to cultivate what we need for trust to thrive.

Markets and Morality

If we take seriously the teachings of neoclassical economics, and the role models of the most successful financial traders, we should put a price on everything that we do, every relationship that we maintain; no criteria should be applied outside that frame. This dispenses entirely with a need for morality or ethics in behaviour. The market is therefore amoral in the strict sense of that term. The issue of trust that we have discussed can be an example of moral behaviour, but not necessarily. When I say 'I trust my doctor, because I believe her to be a good, honest person', I am using trust in a moral sense. But if I say 'I trust my doctor, because I believe that the governing institutions of her profession are highly efficient in guaranteeing high standards of practice', I am talking of a different kind of trust, institutional trust rather than moral trust. The relationship of markets to morality therefore needs a separate discussion.

Few people have done more to explore the ramifications of the amorality of the market than Michael Sandel, in his book *What Money Can't Buy: The Moral Limits of Markets*. He provides some extraordinary examples to show how far the neoliberal idea that buying and selling is the most rational and efficient means of discovering what we should do can lead us away from any attempt to exercise moral judgement. He cites the single mother in Utah who needed money for her son's education and was paid $10,000 by an online casino to install a permanent tattoo of the casino's web address on her forehead. Markets in human organs for use in transplant surgery raise rather larger issues of the same kind. Far more frequent is being willing to serve as a human guinea pig in a drug-safety trial for a pharmaceutical company, where the fee paid depends on the invasiveness of the procedure used to test the drug's effect and the discomfort involved. In the USA, private military contractors recruit mercenaries to fight in Somalia or Afghanistan for $1,000 a day. In a rather different kind of case, children in some US schools are encouraged to read by being paid for each book they read. Sandel also mentions some cases in the USA where drivers who are not members of carpools are permitted to use lanes restricted to carpool members if they pay a fee.

When confronted by lists of this kind, we all have our sticking points as to where we consider the use of money and markets to be acceptable and where not. It might be when people are selling the use of their bodies, or parts of them; it might be when money is being used to compensate for possible mortal danger; it might be when state policing services can be bypassed. There will be debate and disagreement about the issue, and confronting these questions requires us to draw on the wellsprings of our moral sensitivity. Some people may discover that they have none. The point is that we must have these debates and must not look for cop-outs, such as 'the market is always right' – or always wrong. Moral judgements can be disputed. For example, morality may lead to hostile action against people with particular religious beliefs, forms of sexual behaviour or ethnic origins. The moral blindness of the market has rescued many people from prejudice and ill treatment. At the same time, the market will not necessarily operate this way. If a firm wishes to operate in a country where there are deep prejudices against people with certain characteristics, and can only attract customers by following these prejudices, then the market becomes the ally of prejudice. One can never rely on the amoral.

If we follow the strict rules of neoliberal thinking, we should take actions that cost us some effort only if we can give a positive answer to the question 'What's in it for me?', which is a negation of an ethical approach. This approach to life risks eroding the capacity for voluntary and spontaneous generous actions that oil the wheels of social interaction. In reality very few people who in general accept a neoliberal approach want to go that far. This is especially the case for conservatives, whose opposition to the social democratic welfare state and redistributive taxation leads them to align themselves with the 'small state' agenda of neoliberalism, but who are uncomfortable with the amorality and neglect of civil society that follows from a rigorous market approach. Unable to accept that there can be any negative consequences of the work of the market or of private corporations, they have to invent elaborate reasons why the welfare state is to blame for aspects of contemporary society that they do not like.

For example, in the 2012 Reith Lectures sponsored by the British Broadcasting Corporation, the British Conservative philosopher Niall Ferguson dealt with some similar themes. He deplored the decline in voluntary civil activism that some sociologists claim has afflicted the USA, and blamed the strong role of the state in modern society for declining reliance on personal responsibility and civil society. The claim is strange, since today the USA has a smaller welfare state than most western European countries, and the state's role there has been declining steadily since the late 1970s. It is not easy to come by studies that might enable us to place US experience in a comparative perspective. However, the OECD *Better Life Initiative* has tried to measure the quality of life across its member states. The item in its survey that comes closest to Ferguson's topic is called 'Community', and shows the proportion of the population reporting that they have relatives, friends or neighbours they can count on to help if they were in trouble. In fact the figures are very high indeed for most countries, the USA itself standing at 92 per cent. But all countries with stronger welfare states than the USA have levels at least as high, ranging from 92 per cent in France and Sweden to 95 per cent in Germany and 96 per cent in Denmark and the UK. It would seem that neither the market nor the state have undermined some basic elements of civil society.

This analysis of the effects of markets on other areas of life cannot answer our moral dilemmas. Its value lies in showing us the damage that markets do to traditional institutions. This does not enable us to make an automatic negative critique of the role of markets, any more than embracing markets enables us to set moral judgements to one side.

Polanyi and Externalities

The more marketization we have, the more the market's inadequacies are revealed. This is particularly true of the third and fourth sets of inadequacies identified in the previous chapter: public goods and externalities. The other two, inadequate competition and incomplete information, are more amenable to technical solutions. Probably the best way to comprehend Polanyi's arguments in a manner consistent with contemporary economic theory is to see him as showing us the full extent of the meaning of market externality. All those features of society that he sees, for good or ill, being destroyed and not replaced by the market are covered by the idea of externalities. As with all externalities, it is open to us to argue whether that which is lost is compensated by the gain. Much of our following discussion will therefore concentrate on certain externalities that are growing in significance as a result of the current wave of marketization, and on how social democracy stands ready with approaches to overcoming them. This is a somewhat unfamiliar form in which to express social democracy's contribution, which is normally seen by its advocates as being about public goods, in that familiar contest between individual and public (or collective). I do not want to depart from that positioning, but I do want to draw attention to social democracy's value in confronting issues of externalities too. Since this is less familiar, I shall concentrate on it, but first it is essential to acknowledge the continuing importance of public goods issues facing us today.

Problems of public goods loom very large for contemporary societies, particularly those concerned with the sustainability of our way of life. These issues overlap heavily with massive problems of externalities associated with environmental damage and climate change. When we consider these crises as externalities, we think mainly of the role of human action in creating them. Much environmental damage has resulted from perfect examples of externalities: the production of goods for the market, where the environmental damage done has not entered the cost accounts of the firms producing it – though we must always remember that the statist economy of the Soviet bloc contributed more than its share of such pollution. It is important to recognize and to assess this role of human agency in contributing to climate change, because we need to change our way of life and erect different incentives for our behaviour than those being generated by the market itself.

The struggle against climate-change deniers – primarily wealthy US corporations who continue to profit by production methods and products that are continuing to cause damage – is highly important. However, when we think of environmental sustainability primarily in terms of public goods rather than market externalities, we do not even need these arguments. Whatever its multiplicity of causes, climate change threatens the sustainability of human life. To some extent it is beyond our power to prevent some of this threat, but we know that some of our economic processes worsen the problem, even if they did not originally cause it. To do anything about this requires measures going beyond the reach of the market, because public goods are at stake. Our atmosphere is a classic example of a public good in that no one can own it or be excluded from it and therefore no one has an incentive to make money out of looking after it. The market can help with some aspects of environmental sustainability; for example, the development of solar power becomes commercially viable as non-renewable sources of energy become more expensive. But the market tends to respond only slowly to such major challenges. It is only when the negative consequences of environmental damage are actually being felt in our daily lives that market prices are affected, but by then it is probably too late. Only pressure from alert groups in civil society, putting pressure on governments for action, is likely to operate earlier. For the larger issues of how to protect the future of our planet we desperately need action, which, while it might well include the use of the market, must embrace a wider range of measures, in particular the use of state power and a willingness to pay taxes and forego some private consumption.

The complex of issues gathered together here constitutes the biggest single, probably the biggest imaginable, example of the politics of neoliberal societies: there are those who are willing to recognize and act on the limits of market solutions; and those who, because of the interests they represent, always push for more market and refuse to recognize its inadequacies. Today only social democracy has a long political tradition that enables it wholeheartedly to represent the first set of positions. Green parties and environmentalist movements fully comprehend the scope of the issue and become vital allies of social democrats, but are weaker political forces. All other political movements of our period have travelled too far along the road of neoliberalism and dependence on corporate support to be able to be trusted with the sustainability of human life on our planet. Only a coalition of social democratic and green movements can save us. But this coalition also needs to be an international one, as climate change does not recognize the jealous border controls of nation-state politics.

Markets and their Correction: A Complex Relationship

The central positive lesson we can take away from these examples is that marketization needs to be accompanied – but not replaced – by measures that check its negative consequences. The great socio-economic and political confrontations of the past 150 years have been between those wanting more market and those wanting checks on markets, in a kind of zero-sum game. In reality the relationship needs to be and can be a positive-sum one. The process of marketization, as it destroys one set of non-market institutions – often with positive results – needs to be accompanied or rapidly followed by new institutions that correct its own deficiencies assist those values that people find important but which the market is likely at worst to harm (like trust and security) or at best to squeeze into margins if it cannot commercialize them. Meanwhile, it must be conceded, measures that at one time are erected to protect weaker groups from the market can sometimes become protections of privilege for a few, to the exclusion of others. This may require a further dose of marketization, or some other form of intervention to ensure that it does not occur – it was, after all, a routine problem of the pre-modern world before the Great Transformation. This position of accepting many of the benefits of marketization but then seeking actions to compensate for its damage and to achieve goals that the market disrupts is the stance of those who accept neoliberalism of the second kind but are suspicious of the first kind. Nearly all the traditional appeals of social democracy can be incorporated within this overall stance. Citizenship, solidarity, compassion for the poor and disadvantaged, a demand for reduced inequalities can all be reaffirmed by asking what is being gained and what lost by marketization, and if the losses outweigh the gains, what should we do about it. But it is a stance that frames these historic concerns in a way compatible with the economistic reasoning of the present age.

We often manage to achieve positive-sum outcomes between markets and compensating measures for them, but not usually through coherent planning. Rather they come through conflict and confrontation, for reasons explained in the previous chapter. The interests served by intensifying markets and those served by protections from it are usually different, and they are usually distinguished by different degrees of income and wealth. It is probably as well that things remain that way, for conflict and contestation increase our chances of finding new solutions to problems – and of evading rule by benign dictators who claim to be working for us all. It is a central contention of this book that today it is social democrats and green movements that represent the best chance of guaranteeing the vital diversity that comes from admitting that we have no certainty. But before we explore that theme, we must consider in more detail the main classic field of social policy where we can see in action the creative tension between marketization and the measures that are needed to offset its negative consequences: social policy, especially as it affects the labour market.

References

Ferguson, N. 2012. *The Reith Lectures 2012: The Rule of Law and its Enemies.* London: BBC. http://www.bbc.co.uk/podcasts/series/reith

Lütz, S. 2003. *Convergence within National Diversity: A Comparative Perspective on the Regulatory State in Finance.* MPIfG Discussion Paper 03/7. Cologne: Max Planck Institute for the Study of Societies.

OECD 2012. *The Better Life Initiative.* Paris: OECD. http://www.oecd.org/statistics/betterlifeinitiativeyourbetterlifeindex.htm

Polanyi, K. 1944. *The Great Transformation.* New York: Rinehart.

Sandel, M. 2012. *What Money Can't Buy: The Moral Limits of Markets.* London: Allen Lane.

4

Capitalism and the Welfare State

A major historical example of the mixed losses and gains consequent on the spread of modern capitalism can be found in labour markets; this is a policy area to which particular attention will be devoted here. Pre-capitalist labour relations provided security of a sort; ordinary workers could assume that life next year would be rather like this year – barring no unpredictable but entirely possible changes of mind by landowners, no bad harvests, plagues and other illnesses, or natural disasters. (All, in fact, events that were quite likely to take place, but not through developments in the labour market itself.) When various of these disasters did occur there was in most societies an understanding that the wider circle of family members would do what their limited resources made possible to help those affected. We must never lose sight of the fact that the impact of capitalist work relations was eventually to bring many improvements to such a situation, as it brought greatly increased resources. In the first instance however it forcibly disturbed the older securities without replacing them with anything. There were jobs in the new factories, but they were likely often to fail in the unstable conditions of the times, while the growth of capitalism in agriculture opened the old stable poverty to disruption. People often had to move long distances to find work in the new cities, and family and community systems of support broke down. Large numbers of working people were reduced to desperate insecurity and extreme poverty. Eventually, though in different ways and to different degrees in different industries and societies, various new institutions developed to protect workers from this intensified level of insecurity in their lives, eventually doing a far better job than pre-industrial systems ever had. These included public policy measures, such as employment law and social insurance and social security systems, as well as the growth of trade unions as forms of collective action that did not belong to traditional society, the market or the state.

This is the story of how the construction of modern social policy institutions saved people from the brutal rigours of the free market and its destruction of earlier non-market supports, while also improving considerably on those earlier supports. Had the initial marketization not taken place, there would probably have been no opportunity to construct the modern social policies that were so much more effective and useful to workers than the mechanisms of traditional society. Marketization and its corrections can proceed together in a positive way, though it often does not seem like that to those involved in conflicts between the two processes. Today, in the new wave of marketization associated with globalization, which is bringing new levels of uncertainty to workers' lives, neoliberalism is attacking these modern protective institutions, exposing workers to the double insecurity of the intensified market disturbance of globalization and the destruction of employment law, welfare states and trade unions.

The political differences between workers' and employers' interests seem clear here. Employees have an interest in arrangements that will protect them from insecurity, provided such arrangements do not in the end work against their own interests. There may be conflicts between existing employees, who are protected by such arrangements, and those trying to enter the labour market but who are unable to avail themselves of any help or protection. Capitalist employers and managers have an interest in being able to treat labour like any other commodity, as in that way they can maximize their profits. Their interests may seem compatible with those labour-market outsiders who cannot benefit from protection, but employers may simply want to reduce all labour to a position of total lack of protection against insecurity. However, there is scope for compromise here, provided the various different interests are all able to express themselves and wield some power. It is not in workers' interests to maintain forms of protection that make labour markets so inflexible that firms become unprofitable; it is not in trade unions' interests to maintain structures that alienate them from new generations unable to gain access to good jobs. It is not always in employers' interests to maintain rapid hire and fire labour markets that give them no incentives to train and retain qualified staff and earn staff loyalty.

Free markets function best when there are masses of transactions, as these provide the large flows that are needed to set efficient prices. Therefore, from the perspective of neoliberal theory, markets that are sluggish are inefficient. Labour markets in which firms retain staff for long periods – because they attract loyalty and keep their staff well trained – are examples of such 'sluggishness', and receive the disapproval of the theorists. For example, the OECD includes average length of tenure of employees with a single employer as a key measure of labour-market flexibility: long average tenure tends to be regarded by neoliberal labour-market experts as evidence of inflexibility, and scored negatively. This has the unintended implication that firm-specific knowledge and experience are discounted, and firms are viewed positively if they are not concerned with retaining employees, rewarding loyalty or advancing and building on existing workers' skills. Rather, according to this model, employers seeking improved labour input should dismiss their existing workers and seek better ones on the market. These are among the factors that have led the OECD to moderate its approach to labour policy in more recent years. Apart from any other considerations, this approach means ignoring the transaction costs involved in recruiting and developing employees and embedding them in the employing organization.

Protecting from Labour-Market Insecurity

We are here in the classic territory of social democracy, seeking institutions that will protect ordinary people in a capitalist economy, the basic framework of which is accepted, but against the vicissitudes of which such people cannot protect themselves as can the small privileged and wealthy minority. The importance of this basic position is in no way diminished by the fact that some social risks seem to have changed over the years.

We may say that a person has a secure position in the labour market if there is a zero or very low probability that it will be lost and replaced by an inferior one. But does that security mean protection within an existing job or employing organization, or confidence that there is a good supply of equally attractive alternative positions as well as means of accessing them, as well as bringing support during the time of transition, in the event that one does lose one's existing job? The difference is fundamental to current debates about labour security policies, and also exemplifies clearly the difference between defensive and assertive social democracy. Fighting for rights to hold on to existing jobs at a time when many people have no jobs at all, and when technological and market change are leading to the destruction of many firms and job types, is a defensive struggle. In many situations and some entire countries, it is difficult without major changes for workers to see any possibility of achieving anything better than this, though in the end a purely defensive strategy is doomed to fail, unless a crisis affecting a particular firm or region is temporary. In the overall context of major shifts in the activities in which the advanced countries are finding their competitiveness, it does not make long-term sense to try to prop up large-scale employment in old industrial sectors. And in the short term, job preservation for established workers creates outsiders on temporary contracts and other forms of precarious work among younger generations, who then feel alienated from the efforts of trade unions and traditional labour law.

The same problems do not arise with labour policies that provide generous unemployment benefits and help with job search and the acquisition of skills. These market-correcting measures are future oriented and do not create barriers between workers on secure contracts and those in precarious work. Providing a context where workers and their families can feel confident that they will be helped through the process of confronting and accepting change, by their own organizations (trade unions), and by regulation and public expenditure, is a central example of assertive social democracy. Even then, some legal protection against arbitrary dismissal and financial compensation in the case of redundancy is likely to be needed to reduce anxiety about possible job loss; confidence that a new job could easily be found cannot completely replace guarantees that one cannot suddenly lose one's current job. Both approaches (defensiveness and assertive social democracy) differ from neoliberalism, in that they recognize a need to assist workers with the externality of insecurity; but the assertive approach helps construct the emerging changed economy, while the defensive one tries only to resist. Assertive social democracy therefore resembles neoliberalism in its acceptance of needs for change and adaptation in the face of globalization.

Behind insecurity stands a larger concept, the absence of knowledge about one's situation, be it about the labour market in the narrow sense or more generally about the economic parameters that affect one's life. This is the question of uncertainty. Its relationship to insecurity is complex. If one's position is uncertain, it is certainly insecure, but it is possible to be certain that one's position is insecure. However, that kind of certainty is only a certainty that a higher level of uncertainty exists, uncertainty about the likelihood that one's position will improve again. More generally, policies for social and labour-market security can be seen as strategies for helping people who have inadequate knowledge and resources (i.e., most people) to be self-sufficient in their encounter with uncertainty.

This brings us to an important distinction between uncertainty and risk, first established in the 1920s in a much noted book by the American economist Frank Knight. If we can make probability calculations about the chances that an uncertain event will occur, we convert it into risk. In the economic field, probability calculations can be turned into financial calculations. This simple point is fundamental to the entire financial sector of the economy and to concepts of insurance, investment, rates of interest and share prices. Once prices can be placed on risks, people can invest in them, thereby sharing the initial risk widely and reducing the threat that it presents to either the original bearer of the risk or those to whom it has been sold. Uncertainty is never eliminated through this process, but it is shared, and therefore reduced, and can be compensated by agencies who, by taking on a wide range of risks, limit the impact on them of failure occurring in any one of their decisions to accept a share in a risk. Without markets in risk most entrepreneurial projects would be impossible, and the world would be considerably poorer.

But to engage profitably in risk markets requires wealth and knowledge. Wealth is necessary if one's riskworthiness, one's collateral, is to be accepted in the markets. Knowledge is necessary, because the calculation of any but the simplest risks requires considerable information about threats to the risk and the chances that negative events will occur. Information of this kind is expensive to acquire, which serves as a further wealth-based barrier to entry into the risk market for those without a strong asset base.

There are therefore fundamental inequalities in the ability of persons to engage in risk markets depending on their stock of individual (or family) assets. As we know, in all capitalist societies wealth is far more unequally distributed than income, partly because it tends to remain in families for lengthy periods, and does not face competition in the market as does human capital – the asset that produces income and its inequalities. Although the distribution of wealth, like that of income and many other quantifiable attributes, forms a continuum, it is relatively easy to distinguish among:

1. Those with large assets, great enough to protect their level of living against all but the most extreme shocks and to enable them to participate in risk markets that are likely to increase their assets further;
2. Those whose property is mainly limited to illiquid assets (primarily residential property) of which they could not divest themselves without major negative consequences for their standard of living, and perhaps small financial assets insufficient to protect them from any but very minor shocks;
3. Those with virtually no assets at all other than those they need for daily life.

Classic twentieth-century social policies dealt with what have become known as the 'old' social risks: sickness, disability, unemployment, survival past working age, the birth of children. This approach assumed a population coming into the second and third categories, with the great majority being in the third, and therefore unable to be expected individually to adopt the solutions to uncertainty used by people in category 1. These solutions would include taking out major private insurance, and investing wealth into ventures, which, though they carried some risk, were likely (these persons' expensively rewarded advisors could calculate) to bring in a good return, protecting and advancing the level of assets from generation to generation. Instead, the collectivity of the society as a whole (usually a nation state) would provide this cover for the great majority of its members: income protection in the face of major definable risks to a person's economic situation, often using the insurance principle; social policy and often trade union action providing protection against or compensation for dismissal or redundancy; union action and sometimes public policy to try to protect the value of earnings.

Neoliberals and many Third Way social democrats argue that these approaches are no longer needed and can be dismantled. For example, New Labour's long-serving UK prime minister, Tony Blair, used to argue that there was no need for the welfare state to be used to redistribute income and wealth; all that were needed were some measures to deal with the personal and social problems of the very poor. This would be true on either of two conditions: (a) that the labour-market risks no longer existed; or (b) that most persons had both entered category 2 and felt able to behave in the risk markets as though they were members of category 1, leaving only a small minority in 3 needing special help.

But neither of these eventualities occurred. It might be argued that during the period of Keynesian demand management some of these risks were much reduced, fulfilling condition (a), but ironically that period ended at precisely the moment when arguments about the need to tear down some of these protections started to develop. A globalizing economy subject to rapid technological change and alterations in the role and identity of different sectors is hardly one in which the importance of the old risks has declined. A far stronger case can be made out for the contrary position that we have been following here: an intensification of markets requires action to guard against their negative consequences. It is not a decline in the importance of the 'old' risks that has produced powerful campaigns for the abolition of collective protections against them, but the very opposite: people are increasingly likely to need that protection now, but policy-makers fear the costs of providing it, and the wealthy feel sufficiently powerful to refuse to share in the taxation needed to fund it.

As to (b), although the very large rise in general affluence that took place during the second half of the twentieth century did propel large numbers of people from category 3 to 2, this did not mean that they were now indistinguishable from category 1 (i.e., able to confront serious labour-market risk from their own accumulations of wealth and using their own knowledge of investment risks and opportunities). That is one reason why it has been unreasonable for the pensions of middle- and lower-income people to be based on the stock-market performance of their individual assets, as has increasingly become the case and as is discussed briefly below.

The first period of the neoliberal regime from the late 1970s to the early 1990s saw rising unemployment and stagnating wages in those countries that began to adopt the new approach, mainly the Anglo-American world. At that time far fewer labour-market changes were adopted in continental western Europe, nor were reductions made in social expenditure. The initial changes in the Anglophone countries took place following the deregulation of capital markets and the development of sophisticated new financial techniques for risk sharing. These did enable many clearly category 2 people, and eventually even many in category 3, to act *as though* they were in category 1, by taking mortgages representing sometimes more than 100% of the value of residential property. They used the excess on their mortgage debts, not to invest in residential property or other assets, but to sustain their consumption. When people in category 1 undertake debt, they use it to buy assets that will increase their wealth and income. Using debt to fund daily consumption is not category 1 behaviour, and is disastrous. During the same period there was also a major expansion of consumer debt through the growth of the credit card. These high-risk levels of credit were funded through the secondary markets. By the time of the financial crash of 2008, a number of countries had levels of private debt that exceeded total disposable income (a theme picked up by the OECD already in 2005, two or three years before the crash brought the phenomenon home to everyone). Historically, only wealthy persons have carried high levels of debt. (The poor may well have incurred debts that were, for them, crippling, but the actual sums involved were small.) It was distinctive of these very high-debt countries in the early twenty-first century that people on relatively low incomes – the lower part of category 2 and some in category 3 – also incurred high levels of debt.

We now know that the financial markets that drove this system were not based on precise risk calculations. A good deal of the consumption growth that took place from around the early 1990s to 2008 was fuelled by this expanded debt rather than through actual income gains. Adjustment to this reality may well require taking consumer spending in Western countries back to where it would have been had it been powered by income growth unaided by unsustainable credit. This is what is taking place during the current recession.

In retrospect we can see this period of debt-fuelled consumption (what I have called elsewhere privatized Keynesianism) as an attempt to make come true the argument that category 2 people had now joined category 1 in their capacity to deal privately with major financial risk. It failed disastrously, because its foundations were unstable. With that failure also collapses the idea that class inequalities and their accompanying 'old' social risks are no longer important for social policy. Different levels of wealth holding continue to be fundamental in determining whether individuals can now face those risks with their wealth and knowledge resources. The increasing inequality characteristic of the present period intensifies this problem. To the extent that there is a zero-sum game in financial markets, with wealth (and the knowledge on which it can call) enabling its holders to secure the best deals, those lacking in wealth will get the worst deals.

The Problem of Pensions

Pensions policy reveals some of these issues acutely. (This discussion draws on recent studies by Ebbinghaus and Wiß, Neuberger, and Whiteside.) Neoliberals are very concerned to draw attention to the financing difficulties of state and occupational pension schemes in a period of rising longevity. There is also the problem that the retired population includes the large 'baby boom' cohort born in the years after the

Second World War, after which birth rates and therefore eventually the size of the work force contributing to pension funds declined. On 25 September 2003, *The Economist*, the world's leading neoliberal media organ, carried an illustration that became infamous after the crash of 2008. It depicted three pillars (pension systems are usually described as comprising various 'pillars'): one, that was cracked, tottering badly and about to collapse, was labelled 'state pensions'; a second, showing bad cracks but still standing, was called 'occupational pensions'; the third, standing intact and firm was 'private pensions'. Two years later the defined contributions expectations of millions of people enrolled in private pensions were losing value alarmingly, as the funds that had invested heavily in the secondary markets saw their giant bubbles collapse. The 'old' risks that were met by pensions policy – essentially the brutal risk that one might fail to die once one's usefulness to the labour market had ended – have not gone away; they have just become inconvenient.

The case that state and occupational pensions are unsustainable is partly specious. If today the pension-receiving generations comprise many baby boomers while the pension contributors include the generation of declining birth rates, then tomorrow's pension-receiving generations will include the smaller and therefore cheaper to sustain generation of declining birth rates, while the pension contributors will include more of the large generation of the children of the baby boomers. Also, a further cause of a crisis with many occupational pension schemes is that, during the highly profitable stock-market years of the 1990s, many firms decided that the investments of their pension funds had been so profitable and were therefore in such a healthy condition, that they could take a 'pensions holiday'. This meant that for a number of years they made no new contributions to their funds. However, when the bad investment years arrived, they did not decide that they should therefore increase their level of payments, or make up the contributions from the years of the pensions holidays. They simply declared that the pensions fund was in crisis and took such radical measures as reducing the benefits being earned and banning new generations of employees from joining it. None of this means that there are not problems with current pensions systems, or that pension schemes do not need to have a sound financial basis. But the atmosphere of crisis created around pensions, the closure of large numbers of corporate schemes and the exclusion of new generations from those that survive are all testimony to a desire by employers to escape from responsibilities towards employees.

The pure marketization of human labour would leave people completely dependent on making pension provision in the private market. Given the long time horizons of pensions planning, this means that people on modest incomes and having difficulty managing their daily expenditure would forgo making any pension provision until the age of giving up work was approaching and the chances of building up an adequate pension pot past. The result would be deep insecurity and eventually poverty. The market-compensating social policy response in industrial society was the establishment of various forms of national state pension systems and state-regulated occupational schemes. But the market economy itself also gained from this process, as both retired persons and those approaching retirement could be confident consumers of goods and services produced by the private sector. Their consumption was stable and could even act counter-cyclically in the interests of the private market, as, unlike market incomes, pension incomes were not subject to strong fluctuations. Also, pensions contributions from employees and workers provide the financial institutions with large funds, which they can use for their gambling activities in the derivatives markets. However, come the changed power balance of today's neoliberal economy, there are now strong pressures for a marketization of pensions. Further, the financial institutions, whose high earnings are justified by the fact that they bear the risks of pension fund investments, are insisting that pensions be redesigned so that pensioners share those risks. The result is a new wave of insecurity.

Most pre-neoliberal occupational schemes offered pensions based on expected final pre-retirement salaries and wages, so-called 'defined benefits' (DB) schemes. Defined contributions (DC) schemes offer no guaranteed levels of pension income; pensions are based on the investment value of an individual's contributions. These have some advantages for the individual contributor: it is easy to work out what one's investments are worth at any one time, and also to see how much is being removed from one's pension pot as rewards for those administering it. Classic defined benefits schemes are far less transparent in these respects; they depend heavily on trust placed by contributors in the integrity of schemes. This was possibly justified when pension funds were cautious investors, but once fund managers started to enjoy investing in the new secondary markets, this kind of trust became problematic. Once again we see how intensified marketization (the increased market activism of pension funds) destroyed certain taken-for-granted institutions – for good or ill.

But defined contributions schemes throw the market risk of pensions investments on to individual contributors and pensioners and their own investment decisions, sharing risk with the financial institutions who decide how to make the investments and whose profits depend on skilful management of that risk. It is an excellent example of the process, fundamental to corporation-dominated neoliberalism, of a burden being pushed away from financial institutions and on to ordinary people. Individual contributors have to pit their own knowledge against that of the highly informed and professionally advised operators who are in effect competing against them in the markets; the knowledge problem again. And if, as a result of bad luck or poor decision-making, one's investments do very badly, one bears the losses alone, not as part of a risk community as in collective state or occupational schemes.

Neoliberals press for occupational pensions to be 'reformed' in this way, but their preferred option is the abolition or restriction to minimal levels of these pension arrangements, and of course of state pension schemes, in favour of purely individualized ones, whereby people choose pension investment schemes in the open market. Here, instead of a government agency or an employers' organization – both well provided with expertise – negotiating with investors on behalf of pension contributors, the individual stands alone in relations with the investment fund. Ideally, though hardly in keeping with any idea of liberalism, government *requires* its citizens to have such a private pension arrangement, guaranteeing the supply of customers to the funds, but leaves them alone in the market to make whatever deals they can. The leading examples of such combinations of state compulsion and the free market, much praised by neoliberal commentators, are those established in Chile by the Pinochet dictatorship and in Singapore, also by a non-democratic regime. It is more difficult to persuade voters in countries that have elections to accept such coercive arrangements.

It is possible to reduce the problems of defined contributions schemes by having them share risk collectively, within an occupational group or a whole national population; and by ensuring that their governance structures do not place large burdens of risk on to contributors unable to acquire perfect knowledge. A reformed defined contributions system of this kind would meet the standards of reformed neoliberalism. On the one hand, the realities of pension funding in the market economy would be recognized (provided these are not exaggerated) by the move to a defined contributions scheme; but the negative consequences of market insecurity for ordinary working people are recognized in the collectivization of risk and regulated governance.

Reappraising the Labour-Market Reform Agenda

The neoliberal labour-market reform agenda can be re-examined in the light of the wider account of the class inequalities of coping with risk. Under the extreme form of that agenda, individuals become responsible for managing their own employment risks – including what education and training they will need to equip themselves for a changed occupational structure of the future. They cannot expect the state to equip them for labour-market searches or with appropriate skills, because state policy is regarded by neoliberals as able only to interfere inefficiently with markets and impose high tax burdens as a result of its spending programmes. The state therefore shrinks as an agent for reducing uncertainty. But this does not mean that responsibility passes to employers, as under the neoliberal model they too have no duties to assist workers. In the ideal neoliberal labour market there is not even such a thing as employees for whose development firms take some responsibility as a valued resource. There are just individual contractors of labour services offering themselves for hire from time to time and being disposed of when firms will not need them for a while, or think they can easily find better. This part of the neoliberal vision is so unrealistic that it is unlikely ever to be realized in full. There are, however, important steps towards it, in the growth of short-term labour contracts, zero-hours contracts, treating workers as self-employed even though they do all their work for one employer. Firms have increasingly out-sourced their activities rather than take on direct employees. They usually out-source to other firms, who specialize in hiring out labour of specified kinds, rather than to individuals; once again, actually existing neoliberalism represents a game among corporations rather than among the individuals who figure so largely in its rhetoric.

The great majority of workers, including many highly skilled ones, lack the knowledge necessary to know how they should equip themselves with the skills that will be needed in the future. From the perspective of the market, this is not a problem. Provided large enough numbers of people all try different means of equipping themselves for the future labour market, some will succeed, and that may be all that employers need. The rest can be discarded and required to find work available to the relatively unskilled, wasting their mistaken skill investment – such work will exist provided wages are allowed to fall freely until the labour market clears. The same logic is routinely applied to entrepreneurs: many of them try ideas, most fail, but enough succeed to sustain a dynamic economy. Those who do succeed join those whose initial position of wealth exempted them from having to take risks in the first place. And large numbers of those who succeed will do so because supported by the knowledge resources discussed above. The model is one that enhances inequalities as the gap between those who succeed and those who fail becomes wider and self-sustaining.

This pure neoliberal model is very rarely found in real life, but the implicit official stance of the EU, the IMF and the OECD, as well as the actual policy moves of many governments, is that labour-market 'reforms' should move in that direction – as seen in the terms of the Greek bail-out discussed in Chapter 2. The obstinate survival of labour protection is usually attributed to the failure of governments to stand up to vested labour interests. Far less often acknowledged is the rational basis of resistance. Refusal to recognize the importance of the knowledge or information problem of ordinary workers leads the neoliberal approach to generate the externality of a large amount of waste, directly in terms of workers' aptitudes and skills, indirectly in inadequate demand in economies where workers feel so uncertain about the future that they lack consumer confidence, as well as the unpleasant externality of anxiety and fear. Some of these costs may have to be accepted as less important than what is being achieved by the marketization; to some extent market efficiency is simply a matter of abandoning certain objectives in favour of others. In some other cases new markets develop to capture what had been an externality for the first market. In other cases again, however, we may judge an externality to be sufficiently important for there to be a public policy response.

The question then arises of where the cost of that response itself is to be borne. In the classic public policy model the state takes full care of externalities, taxing firms and individuals in order to fund the measures taken. In this way firms are able to keep the profits from their activities and pass the costs of the externalities they create on to other parts of the society. To the extent that corporate shareholders tend to be wealthier than the average citizen, such policy constitutes a shift in burden bearing from the wealthy to the average citizen. This is an argument in favour of progressive taxation, imposing higher tax rates on incomes from profits and very high salaries. More specifically, governments often seek to charge the producers of externalities for at least part of the cost of remedying the externality: for example, the 'polluter pays' approaches to environmental regulation. In the labour market this is the principle behind employers' contributions to social insurance funds. However, if firms are able completely to pass on such costs to customers (or, in the case of labour-related charges, to employees), the measures may remain regressive in their impact. Finally, firms may be induced in various ways to take their own action in relation to externalities, internalizing them. This may result from their market needs (as is the case with company-level training provision and pension schemes); or from the need to achieve deals with trade unions and thereby win good employee relations.

There is therefore no simple formula that relates different interests to policy outcomes, and the contemporary neoliberal climate has generated a variety of responses. The scope for variety is initially established by the sheer lack of practicability of the pure neoliberal paradigm, which proposes ignoring all externalities that are not remedied by markets themselves. Variety is generated further by differences in power relations among employers, employees and their representatives and others in various different contexts, and the availability to the various actors of different means of achieving compromises reflecting their power positions.

As noted in Chapter 1, the search for resolutions to these problems in labour markets within the EU led to celebration of a Danish approach known as 'flexicurity'. This switched the focus of policy from job protection to employment creation, and enabled employers to shift burdens on to the state. Labour protection laws (which protect workers in existing jobs and place the burden of maintaining them on employers) were reduced, though not abolished. The burden of reducing uncertainty for workers was placed on the social insurance system (high levels of unemployment pay) and on help with job search and retraining, shifting the focus of policy to employment security rather than job security and the burdens on to the general taxpayer. General taxation was used to relieve employers of part of their contributions to the system. In contrast, systems with strong labour protection laws, primarily in southern Europe, placed the burden of reducing workers' uncertainty on to employers, who have to retain employees they might no longer need. This is paradoxical, as Denmark is an example of a society with a strong labour movement and social democratic record, and a low level of inequality.

Why did these political configurations with relatively strong social democracy produce a labour-market policy model that has removed a burden from corporations and thrown it on to the general taxpayer, whereas in southern European countries with divided or weak labour movements and high levels of inequality the burden has been left with employers? These are the terms of the social democratic social compromise. Given its acceptance of a market economy and therefore of the need for firms to be competitive, assertive social democracy has to relieve firms of at least part of the costs of maintaining a secure and confident work force, even though they will benefit from having that work force in the long run. (To the extent that firms will benefit from having such a work force in the short run, they can be relied on to accept the cost for themselves.) Under assertive social democracy the state and taxpayers assume most of the burden of compensating for externalities, just as under original social democracy.

To concentrate on the strongest cases, the Nordic countries: despite recent neoliberal shifts across wide areas of policy, their social democratic legacy has given them low levels of inequality, a high level of public expenditure and redistributive taxation and a prominent role for government that has not been fundamentally challenged. The strengthening of corporate power could therefore here result in a transfer of externality management to the state (or rather to a body of taxpayers who were being taxed according to their ability to pay) rather than to a diminution of the state's power. The necessary openness of the Nordic economies has lent power to employers' arguments that they needed labour-market flexibility and help in bearing the costs of providing stable employment. The associated reduction in legal employment rights among employees (except in oil-rich Norway) was made easier to accept by the fact that unions have remained strong, not only at the national political centre but also in individual workplaces, reassuring workers that their lack of rights would not easily lead to arbitrary or unreasonable dismissal. It is possible to argue that the combination of strong union power and a redistributive tax system have helped create trust, which has made it easier for workers and unions to accept both a relief of funding burdens for firms and increased labour-market flexibility. If so, this constitutes an important, if accidental, example of how public policy might buttress both marketization and regulation by mechanisms that support and encourage trustworthiness. This assumption of what might otherwise have been corporate burdens by the state is not an example of the state protection of corporate interests embodied in neoliberalism of the third kind, as here firms' gains from public policy are not parasitical, but part of a reasonable social compromise between state, capital and labour, from which all gain.

The contrasting pattern in southern Europe of high labour protection and low levels of unemployment compensation developed in the immediate post-war context of relatively closed economies, with protected national champion firms, and a relatively small class of employed workers. A high proportion of the population then still worked on the land, and not in classic industrial employment relationships. Although employers bore the burden of strong labour protection, they were in turn protected from external competition, and in any case trade unions and labour inspectorates were often not strong enough to enforce the protection laws that existed; large numbers of workers were, and indeed continue to be, engaged in the shadow economy. The protected part of the labour force was a minority, comprising in general two parts: manual workers in large firms, who might associate themselves with communist movements if not pacified; and public employees, whose loyalty to the state needed to be guaranteed. Pensions, social insurance and labour protection could be concentrated on these groups for political purposes and at relatively low cost.

Industrialization and market liberalization, including the EU single market programme, undermined this 'southern' model. Firms became exposed to international competition and therefore began to object to bearing the burden of labour protection. The movement of rural populations into 'normal' employment imposed strains on social budgets in what remain low-tax regimes favouring the rich in highly skewed income distributions. These systems always protected insiders at the expense of excluded groups, but these latter used to be peasants who remained largely outside modern society. In their absence but in the continuing presence of externalizing policies, a new group of excluded workers has developed: the young, immigrants, women, the old. These now form a large group of unemployed and workers in temporary posts without access to the extensive rights of the protected workers. The southern European social compromise is not working. The wealthy evade taxation in what remain highly unequal societies; increasing demands are placed on social budgets because of the inadequate development of economies, which across many sectors have not developed post-protectionist comparative advantages. The large number of persons excluded from job protection places a further burden on social security budgets. There has been no development of positive-sum exchanges of the flexicurity kind. Instead, temporary and other marginal workers bear the burdens of flexibility, producing segmented labour markets. Meanwhile, the industrial relations and political histories of these countries have produced a context of low trust, in which unions and workers are likely to fight hard in defensive battles to maintain the achievements of the past. They suspect, perhaps correctly, that 'reforms' will bring only a worsening of employees' position without moves to a more constructive new social compromise.

This comparison of Nordic and southern European cases presents a perfect example of the difference between assertive and defensive social democracy. There have been neither strong trade unions nor extensive episodes of social democratic government in southern Europe. During the formative decades after the Second World War when Nordic social democracy established its confident strength, Greece, Portugal and Spain had lengthy periods of right-wing dictatorship, while in Italy the main labour movement party was associated with communism and therefore excluded from government.

We can generalize the themes in this argument further to make the first part of the central claim of assertive social democracy within a capitalist economy: the less inequality there is in class power in the work context and in society in general, the more confident ordinary working people and those who represent them at work and politically can feel that they can advance their interests while accepting change. This means that social democracy can be assertive rather than defensive, leading to constructive developments in social policy. The second part of the claim adds that such a society can also produce economic innovation and success.

That second part requires more argument. It is frequently assumed in policy debates, even by supporters of the strong social policy, that the welfare state might be needed to deal with problems, but that it has to be accepted as a drag and a hindrance of what could be achieved by an economy liberated from such concerns. A major contribution has been made in recent years to European discussion of this theme by advocates of the 'social investment welfare state'. These writers (among them Giuliano Bonoli, Gøsta Esping-Andersen, Anthony Giddens, Anton Hemerijck, Natalie Morel, Bruno Palier, Joakim Palme, Frank Vandenbroucke)

have a very similar project to that of this book: setting out
a model of social policy that is not simply a passive defence
of workers against the vagaries of the market, but which uses
social policy to strengthen competitiveness. In its acceptance
of the need for that competitiveness and of market performance as indicators of success, it is compatible with neoliberalism of the 'second kind'. In seeing value in policies that
amend and seek to structure how markets operate it also
shares our perspective in rejecting neoliberalism of the first
kind. However, in tending to ignore problems of corporate
power and the importance of workers' representation, and
sometimes sharing the classless analysis of 'new social risks'
it departs slightly from our approach by neglecting the
problem of neoliberalism of the third kind, neoliberalism as
corporate power rather than markets. Also, in its criticism
of 'passive' policies (i.e., social benefit transfer payments) it
neglects the important role played in the Scandinavian
systems by generous unemployment pay, which helps workers
accept the risk of job instability in the new economy. Thus
corrected, the social investment welfare state constitutes a
major arm of any future social democratic political strategy.
Welfare states are usually thought of by both their supporters and their detractors as primarily protecting workers and
others against uncertainty – defensive social democracy. The
social investment welfare state also prepares workers for
participation in changing, innovative economic activities. It
is therefore part of an assertive policy, and secures protection
from uncertainty by equipping people to embrace change.

Central to the model is that adult citizens are seen primarily as workers; it is through paid employment that they
acquire their rights in the welfare state. This is true to the
history of the labour movement, which was able to acquire
a political presence for lower social classes on the basis of
the dependence of the whole society on their performing its
work. The Nordic labour movements in particular have continued to insist on the centrality of work as the basis of their
members' strength. This can be contested, though I believe
that it remains fundamental. Until recent years it was not
generally accepted that mothers either should, or should

need, to engage in the labour market. More recently, and especially as global competition seems to make it more difficult for everyone in the advanced countries to find paid work, some observers have questioned the appropriateness of a general insistence on labour force participation, not just that of mothers. Guy Standing, who makes this argument particularly forcefully, also stresses the miserable nature of work for many, perhaps a large majority of, workers. Regular employment requires placing oneself at the disposal of an employer or customer to carry out tasks that are often boring, tiring, difficult and stressful. It is a view of work well captured in the title of a recent study of work by Carl Cederström and Peter Fleming: *Dead Man Working*. Also, the services activities characteristic of much contemporary employment reach further into human relationships than does the manufacture of material goods, marketizing certain person-to-person contacts. This is not in itself at all new; personal services pre-date industrial manufacturing in economic history by some thousands of years, but their importance has increased considerably and raises questions that need to be addressed. Many services sector workers, from medical practitioners to shop assistants, are called upon to present a smiling, welcoming face to all customers, however miserable they might personally be feeling. Most workers in industry and agriculture are spared this.

This makes the case for restoring the improvement of working conditions and work relations to the leading place they occupied in labour politics before Third Way social democrats tried to expel them from the agenda. Work issues remain central to politics and need to be central to political identity. Citizenship rights that are based only on abstract arguments and rhetoric that they 'ought' to exist are always vulnerable to attack from the realities of power. The historical point about the rights established by the rise of labour movements was that they were based on the dependence of economy and society on the products of labour. Our work is needed to make the system work. True, the financial institutions have been trying to create an economy in which money makes more money without the intervention of human labour other than that of stock-market and derivatives traders. But they have failed. Further, it is only if social transfer payments can be reduced by increasing the proportion of adults able to work that the emphasis of public spending can concentrate on the social investment welfare state and the construction of productive infrastructure. For social democrats it should be unacceptable to achieve this by reducing the standard of living of those who have to live on benefits and other transfers. Therefore the numbers of those have to be reduced by more being able to enter paid work.

There is also a more practical issue: the larger the employed work force, the more work is created. This is not widely understood, as it would seem more obvious to believe that there is a given 'lump of labour' that needs to be performed, perhaps a declining lump as improving productivity reduced the amount of labour needed to produce a given output. This thinking leads to policies to restrict the size of the labour force: reduce rather than extend retirement ages; discourage mothers from working; restrict immigration. This was the approach widely adopted in continental Europe during the 1980s and 1990s, and it was disastrous. The cost of early retirement became unsupportable. The continuation of traditional policies for sustaining the 'male breadwinner' model did not prevent women from working but simply reduced the birth rate. It became impossible to prevent immigration, such is the gap between living standards in western Europe and those in the parts of the world from which immigrants mainly come, resulting in illegal populations working in the shadow economy and not contributing to the tax base. As Gøsta Esping-Andersen has shown in *Social Foundations of Postindustrial Economies* (1999), countries that adopted this approach ended up with lower employment levels than two very different kinds of economy that adopted the approach of maximizing the work force: Scandinavia and the Anglophone world, broadly social democrats and neoliberals, with the 'conservatives' in continental Europe losing out. The social democratic Scandinavians expanded their work forces by employing large numbers of women in public employment – the professionals, care workers and administrators of the welfare state. Esping-Andersen believed that the Anglophones, especially in the USA, achieved a similar outcome by having extreme inequalities, so that some people were rich enough to employ large numbers of personal service workers, whose wages were kept low enough (by unregulated labour markets and an absence of unions) to enable the rich to employ even more of them. He regarded this latter model as more viable than the Scandinavian one, as inequalities were likely to continue to grow, while taxpayers would eventually rebel against maintaining the Nordic welfare state.

Esping-Andersen's account was over-simplified. It ignored the dynamism of other sectors beyond public services in the Nordic countries. It ignored diversity within continental Europe, such as French policies for female employment. It exaggerated the homogeneity of the Anglophone world, where really only the USA has such a low level of public service, but it also exaggerated the role of private personal services in the USA. That country also has large numbers of care workers, particularly women, providing services similar to those in Scandinavia or elsewhere. While many are employed in the commercial care sector, many others work for charitable organizations and public service. Esping-Andersen was also not to know, since no one knew at that time, the extent to which American, British and some other countries' employment levels were being sustained by consumption funded by unsustainable debt.

Nevertheless, his key observation remains valid and far more important than these errors: the higher that employment, and particularly female employment, rises, the more work is created. As women enter the paid work force, they need help doing the unpaid housework on which they previously spent much of their time. This ranges from help with child and elderly care and house cleaning to buying packets of prepared salad rather than whole lettuces; whatever it is, it creates paid employment for someone else, usually other women. Should women's male partners share the household chores, the family is still likely to use more paid labour to ease the problems of work–life balance by using the extra income that comes from having two jobs to pay for more services – and to support publicly funded care services.

Paid work creates paid work. It also does this more generally, and not just through these domestic effects, as the more people who are working the more people are spending. Much of this spending goes on in the local economy, creating employment in shops, restaurants and other services. If it is spent on manufactured goods, it might create employment in developing countries rather than 'at home', but employment created in developing countries eventually increases the ability of those people to join in the global economy and buy goods, many of which will be produced in the advanced economies, stabilizing employment there. Further, paid work creates a larger tax base, which provides resources for more public spending, which creates more work and – provided there is a social investment welfare state – a better equipped economy that creates more work.

This is the virtuous spiral of the dynamic, open economy. With the exception of the argument about extending the tax base in order to generate public services and public employment, it constitutes the shared vision of neoliberals and assertive social democrats. Opposed to it are fearful conservatives, traditionalist males, xenophobes and defensive social democrats who see only a limited, threatening world in which a few achievements of the past must be held on to as long as possible. By adding the positive approach to public spending on the social investment welfare state, assertive social democracy shows its superiority over neoliberalism at several points. First, it understands the real contribution that social investment makes to improving economic capacity. Second, by recognizing the need to use some of this public capacity to combat market inadequacies, it produces a more rounded society able to pursue goals other than wealth maximization for its own sake. Third, it is able to create a context of security to reassure those perplexed by social change and globalization, who are likely otherwise to swell the ranks of fearful conservatives, traditionalist males, xenophobes and defensive social democrats.

The agenda of the social investment welfare state includes active labour-market policy, not in the sense of 'workfare', i.e., bullying unemployed people to take any job available, but in providing training and help with job search, perhaps with removal costs. It also includes generally increasing educational opportunities. Several experts in this field immediately think here of specifically vocational education, and it is certainly important to ensure a strong supply of people with skills that have to be specific to their tasks, whether surgeons or bricklayers. But there are also gains from just having a large supply of people who have been trained to think and to use their minds intelligently, as they are the source of the innovation and initiative that can be used to improve performance every day in any job in any sector. It is ironic that current trends to seek efficiency through measuring, targeting and generally directing educational performance drive out those valuable features of a liberal education. Finally and less obviously, advocates of the social investment welfare state also stress the importance of publicly funded child care, to facilitate women's participation in the labour market and to ease the strains of work–life balance on two-career families. Women's entry into paid employment has not only given many women opportunities to lead richer lives and brought many skills into the labour force, particularly those suited to the services sectors, it has also helped with the problem of security. Where both (or all) adult members of a family are bringing home an income, the family can better cope with uncertainty in the job prospects of any one member.

In the following chapter we shall explore the achievements of this approach.

References

Bonoli, G. 2005. 'The Politics of the New Social Policies. Providing Coverage against New Social Risks in Mature Welfare States', *Policy and Politics*, 33: 431–49.

Bonoli. G. 2007. 'Time Matters: Postindustrialization, New Social Risks, and Welfare State Adaptation in Advanced Industrial Democracies', *Comparative Political Studies*, 40, 5: 495–520.

Cederstrom, C. and Fleming, P. 2012. *Dead Man Working.* Alresford: Zero Books.

Crouch, C. 2009. 'Privatised Keynesianism: An Unacknowledged Policy Regime', *The British Journal of Politics and International Relations*, 11: 382–99.

Ebbinghaus, B. and Wiß, T. 2011a. 'The Governance and Regulation of Private Pensions in Europe', in B. Ebbinghaus (ed.), *The Varieties of Pension Governance: Pension Privatization in Europe.* Oxford: Oxford University Press, 351–83.

Ebbinghaus, B. and Wiß, T. 2011b. 'Taming Pension Fund Capitalism in Europe', *Transfer*, 17, 1: 15–28.

Esping-Andersen, G. 1999. *Social Foundations of Postindustrial Economies.* Oxford: Oxford University Press.

Esping-Andersen, G. with Gallie, D., Hemerijck, A. and Myles, J. 2003. *Why We Need a New Welfare State.* Oxford: Oxford University Press.

Giddens, A. 1998. *The Third Way: The Renewal of Social Democracy.* Cambridge: Polity.

Hemerijck. A. 2013. *Changing Welfare States.* Oxford: Oxford University Press.

Knight, F. H. 1921. *Risk, Uncertainty and Profit.* Boston, MA: Houghton Mifflin.

Morel, N., Palier, B. and Palme, J. 2012. *Towards a Social Investment Welfare State?* Bristol: Policy Press.

Neuberger, A. (forthcoming) *A Handbook for DC Pension Design.*

OECD 2006. 'Has the Rise in Debt Made Households More Vulnerable?', *OECD Economic Outlook 2006.* Paris: OECD.

OECD 2012. 'Employment by Job Tenure Intervals'. http://stats. oecd.org/Index.aspx?QueryId=9591. Paris: OECD.

Standing, G. 2009. *Work after Globalization.* Cheltenham: Edward Elgar.

Vandenbroucke, F., Hemerijck, A. and Palier, B. 2011. *The EU Needs a Social Investment Pact.* Opinion Paper 5, May 2011. Brussels: Observatoire Social Européen.

Whiteside, N., 2011. 'Creating public value: the case of pensions' in J. Benington and M. E. Moore (eds.), *Public Value.* Basingstoke and New York: Macmillan Palgrave, 74–85.

5

The Welfare State of Assertive Social Democracy

The claims made in the previous chapter require us to show that egalitarian societies in which employee interests are powerfully represented can perform well economically. This involves looking at some simple statistics comparing various countries. Statistical analyses can disturb the flow of an argument. I have therefore placed them in an Appendix at the end of this chapter, so that those interested can check the facts. Within this chapter itself I shall report the conclusions I draw from the statistics. Because this book is primarily concerned with social democracy in Europe, I shall concentrate on member states of the European Union, together with associate members Norway and Switzerland. I shall not cover the very small states with populations of fewer than one million, as such countries often have exaggerated characteristics (e.g., Luxembourg has the highest per capita income in the world). I shall also not cover the poorest EU members, i.e., those not yet accepted into membership of the OECD: Bulgaria, Latvia, Lithuania, Romania. This is partly because I am mainly concerned with relatively wealthy societies, but partly for the more mundane reason that most of the statistics we need come from the OECD data base, which usually concentrates on member states. I have also added data on the USA, as this is both the largest advanced economy in the world and also often seen as the paradigm case of successful neoliberal capitalism. Unless otherwise stated, the statistics come from 2010, the most recent year for which complete sets are available. This takes account of the initial impact of the 2008 crisis, but not the subsequent crisis in southern Europe.

It was argued in the previous chapter that: *the less inequality there is in class power in the work context and in society in general, the more confident ordinary working people and those who represent them at work and politically can feel that they can advance their interests while accepting change. This means that social democracy can be assertive rather than defensive, leading to constructive developments in social policy, and economic innovation and success.*

To test this we need first a simple means of measuring inequality and employee power, in order to express the most important aspects of class inequality. The most straightforward measure of inequality that has been devised is the Gini coefficient, named after the Italian statistician who invented it. It provides a number that expresses the degree of inequality in a society, so that if all income were received by one, the richest, person, there would be a score of 1.00. Were income to be distributed absolutely equally, the score would be 0.00. Among the countries being studied here the range is from about 0.25 (Denmark and Sweden) to 0.40 (USA). No countries elsewhere in the world have lower levels of inequality than Denmark and Sweden. Several countries, mainly in Africa and other parts of the developing world, have higher inequality than the USA, with scores of over 0.50. Because most of the other numbers being used in the Appendix are expressed as percentages, I have multiplied the Gini coefficients by 100 for ease of reading, so that this range becomes between 25 and 40. Ideally we should like to have Gini coefficients for wealth rather than income, but not enough comparable data are available. We must bear in mind that wealth is considerably more unequally distributed than income.

Expressing employees' power is more difficult. I have chosen to use the proportion of the employed work force in membership of trade unions, as unions continue to be the only autonomous organizations specifically devoted to representing employee interests. It can be argued that membership alone does not indicate the extent of union power, as sometimes they have an entrenched position in a society even when their membership level is low. We shall return to that possibility later, but for now let us make the simple assumption that union power depends at least in part on membership strength.

I am not using indicators of periods in government by social democratic parties as measures of workers' power, as that begs the question of when is a party a social democratic one. It will not be adequate to say 'when it calls itself such', as that tells us nothing about its approach to issues of employee power. We shall, however, turn to the question of the role of parties in Chapter 8.

The measures of inequality and union density for 23 countries are set out in Appendix Table A.1. We can summarize the overall position very roughly by grouping countries into those with relatively 'very high' values (ranks 1 to 6) on a particular variable, 'high' (7–12), 'low' (13–18) and 'very low' (19–23). This gives us the groups shown in Table 5.1 (with countries having very high or very low values on both

Table 5.1. Countries grouped for indicators of inequality and employee power.

A. Relative general employee strength (high union strength and low inequality)	**Denmark, Sweden, Finland, Norway,** Austria, Slovenia, Netherlands
B. Relative general employee weakness (low union strength and high inequality)	**Estonia, USA,** Portugal, Poland, Spain, Greece
C. Relatively high union strength but high inequality	Italy, UK, Ireland, Belgium
D. Relatively low union strength but low inequality	France, Germany, Hungary, Switzerland, Czech Republic, Slovakia

scores in bold type). All groups are labelled 'relative', because they are based on relative standings within the overall set of 23 nations. Dropping one or two countries, or adding new ones, would change the rankings of marginal members of groups. These data can only be used for very broad comparisons.

For measures of economic success we first consider the level of employment. This is central to workers' concerns about their security: can they find work? It is also central to a country's economic success that it can have as many people as possible in the employed work force. Finally, it has been a central contention of neoliberalism that countries with high levels of inequality and weak or no trade unions will be more successful than egalitarian ones at maintaining high employment levels. I take the usual approach of defining the strength of employment as the proportion of the 15 to 65-year-old population in paid work. This leaves out students, but these numbers do not differ greatly across countries.

It can be seen from Table A.2 in the Appendix that there is no evidence that a low level of class inequality has a negative effect in itself on employment performance. Concentrating on the two extreme categories of low and high inequality (groups A and B respectively in Table 5.1), six of the top ten positions for employment performance are occupied by group A countries, only one by group B (the USA). Three countries of mixed strength (Switzerland, Germany and the UK) also ranked higher than the USA, the best performing country in Group B.

Employment levels are an important indicator of the health of an economy, but they do not necessarily tell us anything about innovative capacity. It might be contended that countries with powerful labour interests sustain employment by maintaining stagnant economies, as occurred in the old Soviet bloc. A good indicator of innovative capacity is the registration of patents. It is not a perfect indicator, as patents are more important in some sectors of the economy than others. For example, pharmaceuticals firms make more use of patents than those in the financial sector, so a country with a preponderance of the former will score more highly than one specializing in the latter. However, the indicator has been used as a rough measure of innovation by major international organizations, including the OECD, which collects data for patents deposited in the US, EU and Japanese patent offices. It warns that there is a long time lag in the reporting of patent registrations, and suggests that at the time of writing data are only reliable up to 2002. Only 2002 data have therefore been used in Appendix Table A.1. Table A.2 does the same with these statistics as it did with employment (unfortunately there are no data for Norway or Switzerland). Far from there being evidence that low inequality and strong labour might be associated with poor economic performance, the opposite is the case, the USA being again the only country combining high performance with high inequality and low labour power. The only low inequality country with a relatively poor patent performance was Slovenia, but this country is by some margin the best performing central and Eastern European (CEE) country, as it was for employment.

We cannot use these numbers to claim that low levels of inequality and strong employee power 'cause' high levels of employment and innovation; there are far too many possible intervening variables, and the data are too rough. But they can be used to refute the central neoliberal claim that equality and strong unions destroy jobs and inhibit innovation. Were that claim to be valid, it would be impossible for the most egalitarian countries to have most of the best performances.

It was suggested in the previous chapter that approaches to labour security that depended on strong employment protection laws rather than on generous unemployment pay would be typical of countries with high levels of class inequality. We can now make some check on that. Appendix Table A.1 reports indicators of the strength of employment protection law and the generosity of unemployment pay as calculated by the OECD. Table A.3 produces groups combining these two measures as was done for the inequality and union density measures above, and Table A.4 brings together these two groupings, enabling us to see how countries in the groups shown above in Table 5.1 compare on these two different ways of tackling insecurity.

According to our arguments, countries in Group A in Table 5.1 (labour powerful) should appear in either I or II in Table A.4, depending on whether they have experienced a flexicurity reform process. This is confirmed for all our Group A cases. We should expect countries in Group B (labour overall weak) to appear in IV (weak protection of labour against uncertainty, the pure neoliberal case), unless they have had a history of protectionist regimes, when they should be in III. Poland and the USA are the only cases conforming to the pure neoliberal model. Greece and Spain are in the 'protectionist' box, as expected, but so is Estonia, which is surprising. Of the two other southern European Group B countries, Portugal has higher levels of unemployment pay than we should have expected, while Italy does not have employment protection to the extent we would have expected, though it is only one place off being classified in that half of the table. Our central contention about relations between class inequality and approaches to workers' uncertainty is supported for those cases where the indicators of inequality are clear; the intermediate cases are more complex.

Public policy interest in these issues is concentrated, not on whether different forms of providing labour security are linked to typical levels of inequality, but on their relationship to economic success. Appendix Table A.5 looks at our groupings for labour security regimes alongside employment and patent data, as was done for inequality and union density in Table A.2. The evidence there offers support for the flexicurity thesis, that a combination of strong unemployment pay compensation and relatively weak employment protection laws (Group II) is associated with very high levels of employment. However, there are also strong performances from some countries with 'unreconstructed' regimes with both employment law and unemployment pay high (column I) – in particular from those with low levels of inequality. Contrary to the neoliberal thesis, poor employment performances are concentrated among countries with low levels of unemployment compensation, and it is difficult to decide whether overall the 'protectionist' group (III) performs worse than the preferred neoliberal position (IV). One cannot be highly confident about this conclusion, as cause and effect here are complex; it is likely that countries with high unemployment find it difficult to sustain generous unemployment support. Nevertheless, these data give little support to the thesis that a primarily punitive approach (low employment protection, low unemployment pay) to workers succeeds in maintaining strong economic performance – outside the USA.

Most of the groupings of countries presented here are well known to comparative labour and social policy specialists: similar and usually strong performance among Nordic countries and, depending on the indicator, continental western European countries north of the Alps and Pyrenees; similar and poor performances in southern Europe and in CEE. Research carried out before the 2008 financial crisis showed similar and strong performance among Anglophone countries, represented here by Ireland, the UK and USA; these countries now offer a more mixed picture.

We can take the analysis further by considering further elements of the social investment welfare state. In a contribution to one of the most comprehensive pieces of research to date on the content of that concept (*Towards a Social Investment Welfare State?*, edited by Morel, Palier and Palme), Rita Nikolai has analysed trends in public spending on the three key areas of investment-related social policies discussed briefly in the previous chapter: active labour-market policy (ALMP), family policies and education. She provides data on public spending as a percentage of GDP. All countries we have been discussing are included, except for Estonia and Slovenia. Appendix Table A.6 follows the same format as A.2, showing the ranked distributions of countries across the four groups A to D. Her latest data are for 2007.

In nearly every case the members of Group A (low inequality, strong unions) rank ahead of all those in Group B (high inequality, weak unions), except for the strong performance of Spain in ALMP, and the poor performance of the Netherlands for education. (It needs to be noted here that the Netherlands, like Germany, which scored particularly low for education spending, has a large part of its education system funded by employers in the vocational training system.) The very low position of the USA, with the exception of education, should also be noted. It is more difficult to account for the two uneven groups (C and D).

The high levels for Belgium and France suggest strong state spending traditions not related to the variables at the centre of our focus. We here reach the limits of the broadbrush analysis that is possible with these rough statistics. All systems have their own characteristics that do not fit general stories. For example, France has not performed well on employment in recent years, certainly less well than Germany, and yet it has a considerably higher birth rate than Germany. Among prosperous countries, birth rates tend to be related to economic confidence, and in surveys French couples declare themselves to be more confident about providing for children than do Germans. As recent research coordinated by Ute Klammer has shown, the answer seems to lie partly in the higher level of childcare provision in France, and the greater expectation that mothers will continue to work in paid employment than there is in Germany. German couples face a higher risk of being reduced to only one income than French couples, which affects their willingness to have children. Similar examples of countries not fitting our expected patterns can be found elsewhere. For example, the UK, often considered to resemble the USA in social policy, continues to have a publicly funded health service that American conservatives regard as a symbol of communism.

Coordination and Coverage in Collective Bargaining

We can improve our analysis by giving a better account of employees' collective strength at work than simple union density. In several countries unions occupy an institutionalized role, or are organized in such a way that gives them more strength than implied by density alone. This can be captured in two variables: the degree of coordination of collective bargaining, and its extent of coverage. The former shows the extent to which bargainers can act strategically, pooling together their activities across a number of firms and sectors. The less coordination there is, the more workers depend for their bargaining strength on the market position of their particular firm or occupational group. Coordination, whether among unions or employers, is therefore a form of protection from exposure to the market. The second variable, bargaining coverage, enables us to deal with the fact that unions can often bargain over wages and conditions for a far wider range of employees than their own members. Appendix Table A.1 includes information on both these variables, as calculated for around 2010 in the EU's annual report on industrial relations.

Appendix Table A.7 produces groups across these two variables, as we have done in previous cases. Appendix Table A.8 relates these elements to our earlier account of inequalities of class power. All countries in Group A (Denmark, Sweden, Finland, Norway, Austria, Slovenia, Netherlands), those with the lowest levels of inequality and highest union density, appear in Table A.7's Group 1, where collective bargaining is coordinated and has high coverage. They are joined there by Belgium and Germany. These countries together constitute those that stand furthest from the neoliberal model of industrial relations, but all except Belgium report strong economic performances. Most countries in Group B (USA, Portugal, Poland, Greece), with the highest levels of inequality and lowest union density, have collective bargaining least coordinated and with low coverage. These countries constitute those that stand closest to the neoliberal ideal model of industrial relations, but only the USA has a strong economic performance.

The coordination variable carries a very significant sting in its tail. Important studies of industrial relations systems (especially those by the late Franz Traxler) have shown that there are two kinds of situation in which unions seem to exercise wage restraint, in particular reaching agreements that avoid increasing inflation. The first is where levels of coordination are high; the second is where organized labour is dominated by unions in sectors exposed to high competition in export markets. In the first case, union bargainers whose actions have an impact on wages and therefore prices right across the economy are aware that pressing for high wage rises is self-defeating. Their members' wage rises will also be their members' price rises. In the academic literature these systems of bargaining are known as 'encompassing', meaning that their outcomes encompass large parts of the work force, putting strong pressure on bargainers to have concern for a general interest. In a weakly coordinated bargaining system, individual bargainers do not have to confront the implications of this in the same way. They can push for wage increases for their members without much concern for their impact on the rest of the economy. The export sector factor works similarly. Union bargainers in an industry with strong exports know that high wage rises for their sector are likely to weaken their countries' competitiveness, with negative implications for their members' employment; they therefore bargain with this in mind. These arguments apply to small economies with strong export sectors, exports being a particularly high proportion of overall activity; but also in Europe's largest economy, Germany, through a different mechanism. Here the relevant fact is the dominance of industrial relations by the country's largest union, IG Metall, the union of the metal industries that are so central to Germany's export activities. The German economy is also more dependent than most on exports in the composition of its demand.

These aspects of bargaining coordination are a 'sting in the tail', because they demonstrate an important constraint on the power of organized labour, which is fundamental to the central arguments of this book. The countries in which unions have been most powerful have not been those where their power can be used to defy the logic of a market economy, but to adapt to that logic, while also adapting it to workers' interests by enabling them to be represented in decisions that affect their working lives – a right that neoliberalism reserves to management alone. These characteristics of strong centralized bargaining systems have been known about since the 1970s. They might have been expected to have changed radically since that time, given de-industrialization, globalization and the advance of neoliberalism. In fact very similar lists of countries demonstrate these characteristics and their associated strong economic outcomes. More important for our present purposes, this form of industrial relations conforms closely to what we have called here neoliberalism of the second kind. Unions accept the reality of a market economy, and neither ignore it nor seek to make it unworkable in order to usher in a new social system. But they fight to represent their members' interests within those constraints, simultaneously adapting to marketization while moderating its influence and offsetting some of its negative consequences for the work force. This is a highly important example of how marketization and compensation for its deficiencies can work together rather than in opposition. In this way unions in these kinds of industrial relations system can play the kind of encompassing role that Edmund Burke assigned less realistically to the aristocracy: their particular interests can become a general interest, because their stake in the overall society is so extensive. But unions can only play this role if they and the bargaining system have characteristics that give them incentives to behave this way. The great paradox is that collective bargaining is most able to perform in this market-supporting way when its structure follows neoliberal prescriptions least closely.

In Group A countries, and in a different way also Germany, there is a creative tension between, on the one hand, union strength and/or strong bargaining institutions that give organized labour an important social position, and generous public social policies; and, on the other, strong disciplines that tie the achievement of labour and social goals to the pursuit of strong market competitiveness. The welfare states favour labour-market participation by a maximum number of citizens. Assertive social democracy is not a strategy for hiding away from markets, but for turning reconciliation of them with social citizenship into a positive-sum game.

Extending the Social Investment Welfare State

The concept of the social investment welfare state can be extended to include other areas of public policy, for example the establishment of an infrastructure that will support advanced economic activities. An important characteristic of post-industrial economies is that economic dynamism becomes concentrated in a small number of large urban centres, frequently capital cities (for a detailed account of this phenomenon and the demands it makes on public policy, see the 2006 OECD Report *Competitive Cities in the Global Economy*). This is a paradox, as it was once believed that the freedom from geographical ties of such sectors as information technology would make it possible for them to be located anywhere, unlike manufacturing industries, which often had to be near sources of raw materials and major goods transport routes. But the fact that post-industrial activities can be located anywhere often means that they congregate in a small number of favoured locations. If post-industrial economic development is left purely to market forces, it flows to these places that by chance have particular attractions; other areas suffer from population loss and have no share in economic dynamism. People in search of work concentrate in the favoured centres, usually in numbers far exceeding those for whom work can be provided, as they lack the information that would enable them to make informed labour-market choices; the market for migrants is not efficient. More generally, very large concentrations of millions of people in urban spaces create problems of collective space: accumulation of rubbish and discarded items in unsupervised public spaces, crowding, anonymity, difficulties of moving around, and eventually rises in criminality.

The very rich can protect themselves from these problems of mega-urban collective spaces by constructing private collective areas: gated communities, private police and security services, privileged forms of transport that other urban dwellers cannot afford, private schools and hospital facilities. In addition to buying privilege as such, several of these advantages are devoted to queue-beating, a major issue when large numbers of people are crowded together. An aspect of the current rise in inequality is the growing gap between these metropolitan elites, the harassed lives of the majority of urban inhabitants and the wrecked lives of the smaller number, attracted to the big city by the unavailability of work elsewhere, who fail to find anything better than precarious employment and find no welcoming foothold in the anonymous, unfriendly spaces of the city. The growth of the post-industrial economy has similarly disruptive consequences as the growth of the urban industrial economy that Polanyi described.

The solutions that the capitalist market finds for these problems resemble the answer it found to irresponsible financial markets: for a long time nothing is done at all; problems pile up, but the small elite is doing very well and does not care; until the crash comes. In the big city case the market works by it eventually becoming so expensive to operate businesses in the metropolitan area that firms start to move elsewhere. But this process is very slow to take effect. First, because the elite of business decision-makers has found its own solutions, it responds to the general situation only when it becomes very expensive to hire staff; but as the decline of other regions continues, the supply of new urban migrants postpones this date. Also, locations 'elsewhere' lack alternative attractions, which is why they were unpopular in the first place; there is therefore considerable reluctance to move to them. As a result the move elsewhere does not start until every possibility of extending the size of the original city, with increasingly lengthy commuting journeys, has been exhausted. Meanwhile great costs are borne by both those experiencing the stressed lives of the successful city on only low or moderate incomes, as well as by those left behind in the declining areas of the rest of the country or region, increasingly devoid of facilities and with the liveliest sections of the population having migrated. Very few of these costs, or the transaction costs of the very slow adaptation to growing regional imbalance, enter the money costs of the market economy. They are classic externalities.

Yet again we see how intensified marketization, the process that has helped build the post-industrial economy, requires market-compensating action to prevent discomfort and even disaster. Public policy is needed at several points.

First, if work is to be found only in a few large cities, young people have to leave the potential support of families, communities and friends who might have helped them while they engage in the search for work. They can do this only if there is protection and financial support from social benefits available in their city of destination. But neoliberals oppose these benefits. Indeed, the current frontal attack on unemployment support is coming exactly at a moment when the geographical nature of economic change is making it most necessary. Very cynically, neoliberals will often ally themselves to conservatives who preach the prime responsibility of families and local communities to look after their members in difficulties, in order to argue against government action. (The example of Niall Ferguson's arguments about community responsibility was cited in Chapter 3.) This is cynical, because neoliberalism advocates the very geographical mobility that creates the absence of community responsibility. There is continuing need for the social security policies of defensive social democracy for as long as the process of urban imbalance continues.

Second, big-city life produces many negative collective spaces – crowded, dangerous streets, neglected transport systems, deteriorating areas, a polluted atmosphere – that are classic examples of market externalities. The market can provide solutions only by finding expensive forms of private collective protection for a small minority. Classic public policy is again necessary if more than this minority is to inhabit a pleasant environment; but this requires taxation and public spending. This is another case of the continuing role of defensive social democracy.

Third, the attractions that enable some cities to become favoured for post-industrial development are rarely the pure products of the market. They may have resulted from desirable physical location, or from past public policy – as is the case with most European capital cities, often developed by states over centuries, or areas of past intensive state investment, often for military purposes, as in the case of southern California. Market forces will therefore not suffice either to maintain the attractiveness of an existing large city once size has begun to erode its advantages, or (more importantly) to enable an unfavoured city to make itself attractive. The only solution the market knows for the latter is for wages to fall so far that investment is attracted. The city thrives on low wages and bad working conditions. More proactive policies try to 'market' a city. A city is not a marketable product in the literal sense; it is always an externality. It can therefore be marketed only by analogy, by groups of public and private actors taking steps that will make it an attractive and pleasant place in which to work and live, with a supportive infrastructure and means for producing and/or attracting supplies of skilled labour. City marketing is therefore a case of assertive social democracy, combining public and private efforts for generating collective assets of value to the market economy. There are important examples, discussed in the OECD report cited, of such strategies in the regional economy strategies of the Nordic countries, where governments link their own infrastructure activities with leading firms, universities and other research sites. Geographical attractiveness certainly did not make Finland a major centre for information technology investment; it was the result of hard and imaginative work bringing together public and private entrepreneurialism.

References

Ahles, L., Klammer, U. and Wiedmeyer, M. 2012. *Labour Market Insecurities of Young People and Family Formation. France and Germany Compared.* Unpublished GUSTO paper.

Klammer, U. and Letablier, M.-T. 2007 'Family Policies in Germany and France: The Role of Enterprises and Social Partners', *Social Policy and Administration*, 41, 6: 672–92.

Morel, N., Palier, B. and Palme, J. 2012. *Towards a Social Investment Welfare State?* Bristol: Policy Press.

Nikolai, R. 2012. 'Towards Social Investment? Patterns of Public Policy in the OECD World', in Morel et al. (eds.), q.v.

OECD 2006. *Competitive Cities in the Global Economy.* Paris: OECD.

Traxler, F., Blaschke, S. and Kittel, B. 2002. *National Labour Relations in Internationalized Markets.* Oxford: Oxford University Press.

Traxler, F., Brandl, B. and Glassner, V. 2008. 'Pattern Bargaining: An Investigation into its Reasons, Causes and Evidence', *British Journal of Industrial Relations*, 46: 33–58.

Appendix to Chapter 5

Table A.1. Measures of inequality and employment statistics for 23 countries.

1	2 2010 %	3 2010 %	4 2010 %	5 2002	6 2008	7 2008	8 2010 %	9 2010 %
Austria	29.1	29.1	71.7	0.0286	1.93	62	93	85
Belgium	33	51.9	62.0	0.0282	2.18	65	46	82
Czech R	25.8	17.4	65.4	0.0014	1.96	55	25	36
Denmark	24.7	68.8	73.4	0.0336	1.5	75	44	73
Estonia	36	6.7	61.0	0.0000	2.1	35	40	18
Finland	26.9	67.5	68.1	0.0377	1.96	70	40	78
France	32.7	7.6	64.0	0.0294	3.05	61	20	82
Germany	28.3	18.8	71.1	0.0547	2.13	62	50	55
Greece	34.3	24	59.6	0.0008	2.73	23	30	42
Hungary	30	16.8	55.4	0.0026	1.65	51	24	29
Ireland	34.3	36.6	60.0	0.0110	1.11	75	46	36
Italy	36	35.1	56.9	0.0105	1.89	9	34	59
Netherlands	30.9	21	74.7	0.0607	1.95	73	57	71
Norway	25.8	53.3	75.3		2.69	73	50	68
Poland	34.9	15	59.3	0.0003	1.9	48	23	29
Portugal	38.5	19.3	65.6	0.0006	3.15	61	35	34
Slovakia	25.8	17.2	58.8	0.0004	1.44	39	50	34
Slovenia	31.2	26.6	66.2	0.0056	2.51	67	45	77
Spain	34.7	15.9	58.6	0.0036	2.98	48	38	70
Sweden	25	68.8	72.7	0.0581	1.87	67	51	82
Switzerland	33.7	17.8	78.6		1.14	73	28	43
UK	36	27.4	69.5	0.0213	0.75	61	12	28
USA	40.8	11.9	66.7	0.0452	0.21	32	18	12

Column key:
1 = country
2 = Gini coefficient
3 = union density (% of employees in membership of trade unions)
4 = employment (% of population aged 15–65 in some form of paid work)
5 = patents (index of number of patents registered at European, Japanese or US patent offices in a ratio to population)
6 = strength of employment protection laws (according to index constructed by OECD)
7 = unemployment pay replacement level (according to index constructed by OECD)
8 = collective bargaining coordination (according to index constructed by Jelle Visser at ICTWSS)
9 = collective bargaining coverage (according to index constructed by Jelle Visser at ICTWSS)

Appendix

Table A.2. Ranked employment and patent levels by Table 5.1 categories (see p. 93).

Employment				Patents			
A	B	C	D	A	B	C	D
			CH	NL			
NO				SE			
NL							DE
DK					USA		
SE				FI			
AT				DK			
			DE				FR
		UK		AT			
FI						BE	
	USA					UK	
SI						IE	
	PT					IT	
			CZ	SI			
			FR		ES		
		BE					HU
	EE						CZ
		IE			EL		
	EL				PT		
	PL						SK
			SK		PL		
	ES				EE		
		IT					
			HU				

Country key: AT = Austria; BE = Belgium; CZ = Czech Republic; DK = Denmark; EE = Estonia; FI = Finland; FR = France; DE = Germany; EL = Greece; HU = Hungary; IE = Ireland; IT = Italy; NL = Netherlands; NO = Norway; PL = Poland; PT = Portugal; SK = Slovakia; SI = Slovenia; ES = Spain; SE = Sweden; CH = Switzerland; UK = United Kingdom; USA = United States of America.

Table A.3. Countries grouped by means of addressing labour protection.

I. General high protection (high EPL and high URL)	Norway, Slovenia, Belgium, France, Portugal, Finland, Netherlands, Germany
II. High URL, low EPL	Switzerland, Denmark, UK, Ireland, Austria, Sweden
III. Low URL, high EPL	Greece, Spain, Czech Rep., Estonia
IV. General low protection (low EPL and low URL)	USA, Slovakia, Italy, Hungary, Poland

EPL = strength of employment protection laws
URL = level of unemployment replacement pay

Table A.4. Countries grouped on class inequality (A–D) and labour protection (I–IV) variables.

	I	II	III	IV
A	Finland, Netherlands, Norway, Slovenia	Austria, Denmark, Sweden		
B	Portugal		Estonia, Greece, Spain	Poland, USA
C	Belgium	Ireland, Switzerland, UK		Italy
D	France, Germany		Czech Rep., Slovakia	Hungary

Appendix

Table A.5. Ranked employment and patent levels by Tables A.3 categories.

Employment				Patents			
I	II	III	IV	I	II	III	IV
	CH			NL			
NO					SE		
NL				DE			
	DK						USA
	SE			FI			
	AT				DK		
DE				FR			
	UK				AT		
FI				BE			
			USA		UK		
SI					IE		
PT							IT
		CZ		SI			
FR						ES	
BE							HU
		EE				CZ	
	IE					EL	
		EL		PT			
			PL			SK	
		SK					PL
		ES				EE	
			IT				
			HU				

Country key: See Table A.2.

Table A.6. Public spending on social investment welfare state.

ALMP

%	A	B	C	D
1.3	DK			
1.2			BE	
1.1	NL, SE			
0.9	FI			FR
0.7	AT	ES		DE
0.6	NO		IE	CH
0.5		PL, PT	IT	
0.3			UK	CZ, HU
0.2		EL		SK
0.1		USA		

Family policies

%	A	B	C	D
3.5				HU
3.4	SE			
3.3	DK			
3.2			UK	
3.0				FR
2.8	FI, NO			
2.6	AT		BE, IE	
2.0	NL			CZ
1.8				DE, SK
1.4			IT	CH
1.3		PL, ES		
1.2		PT		
1.1		EL		
0.7		USA		

Education

%	A	B	C	D
6.6	DK			
6.1	SE			
5.9			BE	
5.5	FI			FR
5.4	NO			
5.2			UK	
5.1	AT	PT		CH
5.0		USA		
4.9				HU
4.8		PL		
4.7	NL			
4.4			IE	
4.2		ES		
4.1			IT	CZ
4.0		EL		DE
3.4				SK

Country key: See Table A.2.
Figures indicate percentage of GDP devoted to public spending on policy area concerned in 2007 (Source: Nikolai 2012).

Table A.7. Coordination and coverage in collective bargaining.

1. High coordination, high coverage	Austria, Belgium, Denmark, Finland, Germany, Netherlands, Norway, Slovenia, Sweden
2. High coordination, low coverage	Estonia, Ireland, Slovakia
3. Low coordination, high coverage	France, Italy, Spain
4. Low coordination, low coverage	Czech Republic, Greece, Hungary, Poland, Portugal, Switzerland, UK, USA

Table A.8. Countries grouped on class inequality (A-D) and industrial relations (1–4) variables.

	1	2	3	4
A	Austria, Denmark, Finland, Netherlands, Norway, Slovenia, Sweden			
B		Estonia	Spain	Greece, Poland, Portugal, USA
C	Belgium	Ireland		Italy, Switzerland, UK
D	Germany	Slovakia	France	Czech Republic, Hungary

References

Nikolai, R. 2012. 'Towards Social Investment? Patterns of Public Policy in the OECD World', in Morel et al. (eds.), q.v.

OECD, various years. http://www.oecd.org/statistics.

Visser, J. 2011. *Data Base on Institutional Characteristics of Trade Unions, Wage Setting, State Intervention and Social Pacts, 1960–2010 (ICTWSS)* Version 3.0. Amsterdam: Amsterdam Institute for Advanced Labour Studies.

6

Confronting Threats and Enemies

The most important conclusion that we can draw from the previous chapter is that assertive social democracy is not some dream or remote vision, but an ongoing reality, an actual achievement, primarily in a small but important part of the world, north-western Europe. One might then expect to find attempts by other countries, at least within Europe, to converge on to this model. Instead however we find that, despite the continuing success of these egalitarian welfare states, they are themselves starting to acquire the characteristics of either the neoliberal or the merely defensive social democratic models. Income inequalities are rising, numbers of young workers on temporary contracts are increasing, and union membership and collective bargaining coordination and coverage are declining – almost everywhere. North-western Europe is sharing fully in this experience, though it remains the most egalitarian region of the world; and its relative position has not changed much, because things have deteriorated even further in other countries. Local elites in these countries today very rarely draw attention to the positive aspects of their successful characteristics, only the restraining influence they have on the pursuit of free markets and unchallenged managerial dominance in the firm. This is not surprising, as these elites have seen their counterparts in the USA and elsewhere in the world enjoying high levels of inequality of power and income, and would rather like to imitate them.

We are faced with the paradox that, while assertive social democracy is clearly associated with features that look forward to a more successful, egalitarian world, enabling the populations of the old post-industrial societies to renew their competitiveness while not losing their important past gains of reducing uncertainty, it is in danger of becoming a world that we have lost before most of us attain it. The reasons for this are complex. At one level, demographic changes – mainly population ageing – are increasing the share of welfare state expenditure devoted to transfer payments, primarily pensions, leaving less available for either active labour-market policy or infrastructure development. There are sound solutions for this in current policy moves for postponing official retirement ages and trying to maximize the proportion of the adult population in paid employment. It remains true, as discussed in Chapter 4, that the more people who are in work, the fewer benefits need to be paid and the broader the taxation base of the population for funding the welfare state. Further, as also discussed in that chapter, there is a relationship between publicly funded child care and the size of the work force in the next generation. The better the child care, the more mothers can work; the more mothers work, the broader the tax base, but also the higher the birth rate; the higher the birth rate, the more workers and taxpayers in fifteen to twenty years' time. Immigration is also helpful, as immigrants tend to be of working age and have high rates of labour force participation; they improve the ratio between taxpayers and dependants. But high rates of immigration clearly bring stress to some sections of the native population, which is exploited by right-wing xenophobic and nationalist movements. There is, however, evidence that these stresses are better contained in societies with strong welfare states, as these provide a cushion of security that reassures low-skilled members of home populations (see the work of Antonio Martín and Guglielmo Meardi).

The decline taking place in trade union membership is a major concern. In several countries, in particular Germany and the Netherlands, high levels of coordination and bargaining coverage are sustaining well-functioning industrial relations arrangements despite this decline; but this is a dangerous route for unions to follow, as it gives them responsibility without power. While governments and employers continue to understand the utility of strong bargaining institutions, they will be willing to keep them in place. But there is a cost for employers, as they have to accept that employees have a right to representation and they must share information with those representatives. They often envy their counterparts in the USA who, outside a small number of sectors, face no such constraints on how they treat their employees. If unions depend only on their past institutional achievements, unsustained by present membership power, for their social role, they are at risk of seeing those achievements whittled away. The beginnings of this can be seen in the growing number of temporary workers, not only in the countries of southern Europe, but also in Germany, the Netherlands, and increasingly the Nordic countries.

The unions' membership problem is no longer, as it was in the 1980s, that they primarily represent male workers in declining manufacturing industries. In all advanced countries except Austria and Germany unions today have a majority of women members; and their main sector is public services, not manufacturing. The two aspects are closely related, as women dominate employment, particularly junior levels, in public services. Unions' principal need is to gain members in private services, and also generally among young people. While public employment provides a valuable base for unions as parts of the social democratic movement, linking as it does their membership's professional interests with the social policy and care services that are central to social democracy's central concerns, it also presents a danger. If social democratic governments sustain good employment and bargaining rights for public employees while these conditions are declining throughout the private sector, public employees become a privileged *cadre gardé* for social democracy, leading to resentment among other workers and also to a weakening of a major claim of social democracy to occupy the moral high ground in politics as the movement that opposes privilege and stands for universal rights. Also, as we saw in the previous chapter, union strength plays a constructive role within a market economy only when it is encompassing.

For neoliberals the answer to this problem is to destroy union membership and also good employment conditions in the public sector – the achievement of which is a major objective of policies of privatization and contracting out public services. The social democratic response has to be to bring private standards up to the level of public ones, including the spread of union membership and representation in private services. This must include representation of temporary workers and of those forced into false self-employment and other precarious positions. Again, failure to do this would lead to unions representing relatively privileged insider groups, whether public or private, to the exclusion of those most vulnerable in work relations and therefore most in need of representation.

Employer opposition, especially in relatively small workplaces and among precarious workers, is a major reason for the failure of unions to recruit in many private services. Social democratic governments need to introduce legislation that protects individuals' rights to join unions and to demand union recognition in their place of work. A reasonable *quid pro quo* for this would be action by unions, with employers, to develop forms of coordination and coverage that enable collective bargaining to be sensitive to market needs, as discussed in the previous chapter.

Another issue, however, is that the organizational form of unions, like many other types of association inherited from the nineteenth and twentieth centuries, is not attractive to people today. This type of association establishes a formal membership relationship with a subscribing member, with the member acquiring rights to participate in discussions, decisions and elections. The association itself takes the form of a bureaucracy, but headed by elected officials. The model only really works in small structures, where the promise of participation is easily fulfilled. This long ago ceased to be the situation in modern mass organizations. People retained membership because it was part of the culture of the workplace and industry concerned, but it was far more difficult to carry the model over to new sectors that developed with the radical structural changes of the past three decades. Younger generations of workers have developed different means of connecting their lives to the wider public arena, through more flexible and transient organizational forms, social media and other electronic forms of communication.

Unions, like many other similarly affected associations, are learning how to use new communications media, and it is possible to organize campaigns and conflict actions through them, but they do not necessarily bring dues-paying members. In an ironic way it almost seems as though the cultural habits of early twenty-first-century people are returning organizational activity to the late nineteenth-century forms of French anarcho-syndicalism. Under this model, a union or other conflict organization did not need many members, just a core of dedicated *militants*, provided it could call on far larger numbers to rally round when a call to action was issued by the leadership. Had Facebook existed in nineteenth-century France, the anarcho-syndicalist unions would have been among its main users. But unions built on this pattern could not solve the problem that the lack of dues-paying members meant an absence of serious resources. Compared with their counterparts in Austria, Germany, Belgium and the Netherlands, the Nordic countries or the UK, French unions remain today without the resources to do the technical and organizational work that they need – especially if they are to play the kind of responsible, market-regarding role described in the previous chapter. The 'return' to loose organizational attachments heralded by movements based on social media is therefore particularly untimely for this purpose.

It is possible that solutions to this dilemma could be found in the unlikely sources of two very different nineteenth-century organizational forms. These were both reflections of the weakness of the early labour movement; but weakness is again a problem.

First, unions need means to reach workers, especially but not only young ones, who do not have jobs in the large firms and public service organizations within which unions have become accustomed to concentrate their communications with members. The new precarious work force finds itself in small, sometimes ad hoc organizations, or with no identifiable employer at all. If they do have an employing organization, they are likely to stay with it for only brief periods. The early unions, which had similar problems, found their members in their neighbourhoods and communities. And if they could not do much for them through collective bargaining and representation because of employer opposition, they looked to their other needs. Many nineteenth-century unions were linked to burial societies, helping very poor workers reduce the costs on their families of disposing of their dead bodies. Different, hopefully less gloomy, services might be provided by today's unions. For example, some Italian unions already offer help with completing annual income tax returns. If an important characteristic of contemporary life is the erosion of barriers between the worlds of work and social life, there should be opportunities of finding such examples, such as union childcare for working mothers.

Second, and very different, is the model of the Austrian labour chamber. There are compulsory chambers of commerce for firms in a number of continental European countries, themselves a mixed legacy, partly of old German guild traditions, partly of Napoleonic modernization and rational order. Firms are required to pay a subscription to belong to them, and they have an official role, governments being required to consult them about public policy issues. But their internal governance is autonomous, their leaderships being elected by the member firms. They have a geographical basis, with local, regional and national levels, and represent all economic activities in their areas; therefore they do not lobby for specific sectors, unless a sector is dominant in an area. They also provide a level playing field for all firms, rather than an opportunity for privileged influence by a favoured few, as in the corporate lobbying model. It is of course highly unpopular among neoliberals, but survives and is finding new roles as channels for tackling issues of geographical imbalance in economic development as discussed in the previous chapter.

Only in Austria is there an equivalent institution on the employees' side, though in the past some pre-neoliberal German conservatives considered the possibility of imitating it. The labour chambers have the duty of representing the interests of all manual and non-manual employees (*Arbeiter und Angestellte*). They can draw attention to issues, and governments are required to consult them. As with the chamber of commerce model, they are funded by compulsory deductions from members (in this case from employees' pay), but are self-governing. They are not permitted to engage in conflict actions or associate themselves with particular political parties. A creation of the Hapsburg empire, the chambers are seen by left-wing critics as state-dependent rivals to unions, unable to call strikes but likely to steal unions' thunder by being the official representatives of workers' interests on a number of issues. In practice they have developed good relations and an understood division of labour with Austrian unions. They have, however, usually been seen as a quaint, typically Austrian anachronism by most observers of industrial relations.

It may be time to revise this view. While unions are in danger of becoming restricted to a declining core of stable employees in a few sectors, the chambers have been pursuing the problems of workers in precarious positions. In addition to participating in discussions with governments and employers, they have recently developed new means of addressing the large numbers of young workers who stand outside stable employment – for example by engaging in joint activities with the Viennese alternative newspaper *Der Falter*. It is notable that temporary employment has not been growing as rapidly in Austria as in neighbouring countries with similar employment protection regimes. Would such institutions, adapted to take a non-bureaucratic stance, using social media to encourage mutual communication between organizations and workers, help other countries to reduce the problem of labour-market outsiders, and to work alongside but complementary to unions to bridge gaps in labour-market representation?

The Threat from the Corporate Rich

But beyond these demographic and organizational issues, the principal barriers to the progress of assertive social democracy are political. Capitalist elites in northern Europe not only envy the power in the workplace of their US counterparts; they also envy the high and increasing level of inequality in that country, which is a combined result of extremely high incomes at the top and low levels of redistributive taxation, the latter being in turn the consequence of a poorly funded welfare state and public infrastructure. In addition, globalization gives rich individuals and corporations an ability to locate themselves for fiscal purposes in tax havens around the world. Globalization does not mean, it must be noted, that it is no longer profitable to produce goods and internationally traded services in northern Europe. The skilled work forces and high-quality infrastructures of the region continue to make it competitive; otherwise, how could Germany enjoy a positive trade balance with the rest of the world, while the USA has major trade deficits? Rather, the great corporations and rich individuals no longer want to contribute to the taxes that make possible that skilled labour and strong infrastructure. They just want to profit from these features – products of earlier generations' greater willingness to tackle market inadequacies and provide public and collective goods.

The Problem of the EU and the USA

Because globalization is so important to the changing balance of power between capital and the rest of the population, it is tempting for the left to imitate the increasingly popular xenophobic right and seek a return to nationalism and economic protectionism. It is an important aspect of the unbalanced nature of politics in post-democratic societies that the nationalist right is often an actual or potential political partner for neoliberals – whether in coalitions, as has occurred in the Netherlands, or as part of the same party, as with British Conservatives and US Republicans. Neoliberals are the main sponsors of globalization, and their policies imply high and unrestricted cross-national interaction, including high levels of immigration. They therefore do not share the xenophobic agenda, but find it useful to divert criticism from the interests that they represent themselves. Immigrants and international organizations can absorb the blame that might otherwise fall on global corporations.

Economic nationalism would be a more logical response from social democratic movements, but it is a temptation that they must resist. This is partly because blaming immigrants and foreigners is to pick on targets who are not responsible for the economic problems presented; and also because protectionism is a dangerous trap. Protectionism involves preventing domestic consumers from having access to goods produced abroad, through either outright import bans or heavy tariffs. Once a country does this, its trading partners retaliate. Advocates of economic nationalism and opponents of globalization therefore have to contemplate a general decline in international trade and a considerable reduction in consumer choice. Domestic producers then enjoy a considerable decline in competition; and with this come declining incentives to innovate or to bother to please customers. The quality of goods and services declines. Consumers try to evade controls in order to buy superior goods from countries where quality has been maintained, so a policing network has to be developed to control their behaviour. If the domestic firms are in the private sector, the growth of politically privileged economic elites, one of the main problems of actually existing neoliberalism with which this book is concerned, becomes much worse, not better. If production is taken over by the state, the incentives to provide quality and satisfy consumers become even lower, because there is monopoly. If a country ever wants to come out of this spiral of declining quality, it faces the problem that its poor-quality products must suddenly face competition from superior ones from countries that remained within globalization. Domestic producers are then likely to go into major crisis, and the economy will end up with far more exposure to forces beyond national control than before, as whole sectors become largely imported. That is what happened to the economies of the state socialist system.

It would therefore seem that we face a choice between on the one hand accepting globalization and its associated transfer of power and wealth to an international capitalist elite that lies beyond the reach of democracy, and on the other establishing regimes of national protection, which transfer power and wealth to local capitalist elites, who provide us with poor quality goods and services until they collapse and we are exposed to globalization more virulently than before. There is, however, a third possibility, which has to be embraced by social democrats, and indeed by anyone else who rejects both extreme neoliberalism and a retreat into protectionist nationalism: to build supranational structures that are capable of representing interests beyond market forces and global corporations.

These structures do exist in a weak form, but given the prevailing politico-economic power of neoliberal capitalism, they operate primarily as agents of rather than as checks to that power. There is the World Trade Organization, the IMF, for poor countries the World Bank, for advanced countries the OECD, for Europeans the EU. We noted in Chapter 1 how some of these organizations had recently amended their extreme neoliberalism of the 1980s and 1990s, when they had advocated uncompromising and almost unthinking deregulation. They are also capable of taking on a regulatory agenda that embodies more than market-making. The OECD has a strong programme countering corruption in relations between big business and governments – an agenda shared by social democrats and pure-market neoliberals, but not by the corporate power neoliberals of the third kind. The World Bank has begun to take poverty and the establishment of infrastructure seriously. The WTO is a bigger problem, as it has the purely neoliberal agenda of monitoring governments' adherence to rules of free trade. Countries are permitted to join the WTO and enjoy the benefits of easy access to world markets only if they themselves follow free-trade principles. It would, however, be entirely possible to add certain social clauses to its membership criteria, in order to prevent countries permitting slavery, child labour, unsafe and unhealthy basic working conditions, or other inhuman practices, from joining the free-trade regime.

Such a step is necessary, for otherwise, by demanding free trade and nothing else, WTO rules actually encourage firms and countries to engage in bad labour and environmental practices as easy routes to competitive success. There is no possibility of neutrality here; either an international regulatory regime rejects the importance of all market inadequacies and externalities by insisting on pure markets, or it recognizes that markets can cause harm as well as good. One way to do this would be for the WTO to adopt as its membership criteria the labour codes agreed by the ILO, which is an organization that represents governments (but also employers and unions) just as does the WTO itself. There is a problem here, identified by Guy Standing, in that in recent years neoliberal pressure has also led to a weakening of many ILO conventions, but the mechanism is there. What is lacking is the political will among the governments of the world, under the influence of leading corporations who are quite relaxed about taking their profits from human misery. But it is important to point out that the problem is purely political, not technical. The instruments exist, and if governments care enough about an international issue they are able to produce the cooperation needed to use them. This was shown very clearly after the terrorist attacks on New York City in September 2001, after which levels of regulation of cross-national financial transactions were introduced that governments, including that of the USA, usually claim to be impossible when the issues concerned are those of tax evasion.

In this context we can examine the role of the European Union in forging an agenda of this kind. The primary purpose of European integration has always been the making of markets; but there has also been a distinct if subsidiary role for externality-correcting social policy. The initial, 1950s common-market project was primarily about breaking down barriers to trade, and therefore a marketization project. But there were social policy themes too: a general commitment to 'ever-greater union', and an agricultural policy that was concerned with farmers' welfare. Also, one or two European-level policies were aimed at preventing any downward spiral in social policy that might follow intensified international competition; but there was not much else. In general, social policy was left to the member states. This was important for them, because they were constructing national welfare states as part of their democratic legitimacy with their citizens.

A big expansion in social policy ambitions took place alongside the Single Market project of the early 1990s, coinciding with the Delors and later Prodi presidencies. This was a classic example of what is being advocated in this book: a market-strengthening project being accompanied by social policy measures designed to balance certain limited externalities of the market strategy, and to prevent a 'race to the bottom'. The achievements of the period were impressive compared with the preceding forty years but limited in their eventual scope. This can be attributed to the fact that, from the mid-1990s onwards, a new and sharper edge developed for the market-making strategy. Attention was now focused on labour markets and their related social policy, not to prevent races to the bottom, but to encourage them. There was anxiety about a lack of European competitiveness in relation to the USA, where there are few labour rights, weak trade unions and a poor-quality welfare state. Soon afterwards came the accession of new member states, primarily from central and Eastern Europe, where many governments and newly emerging elites wanted to move as far as possible from anything resembling the state–socialist model and therefore sought strong doses of unregulated marketization. The EU embarked on a major new marketization drive, including seeking the privatization of, and subsequent cross-national competition in, public services.

The logic of market compensation running alongside intensified marketization was not completely abandoned, however. The success of Danish and Dutch combinations of an intensified marketization of labour with the development of certain kinds of labour rights led to an interest in active labour-market policy. At the same time other international organizations that had championed the marketization agenda (especially the OECD and World Bank) began to respond to the logic of the need for externality-counteracting measures, partly to ensure the sustainability of the market economy itself, including trying to check the move to ever-greater inequality. However, as we saw in Chapter 1, when the crisis of Greece and other southern European countries broke, the Commission, the European Central Bank and the IMF moved rapidly back to extreme marketization policies. At the same time, decisions in the European Court of Justice in particular have seemed to be dismantling social policy and trying to reduce the role of collective action in the labour market. The EU is emerging again as a force for marketization, but more aggressively than in the past. Previously it tolerated and accepted national-level social policy; today it is attacking attempts to protect social policy at that level while not developing its own.

As should have been predicted, workers negatively affected by this intensified marketization drive have reacted. From Greece to Sweden the response has been to seek to defend national social policy institutions against the European challenge. The response is purely defensive, because building new policies to defend labour interests at national level means a flight from the reality of globalization. Splitting the marketization and compensatory agendas across the European and national levels respectively will only inhibit the construction of balanced policy in Europe. The dice are already loaded against a balanced strategy by growing socio-economic and political inequality in virtually all societies. Social democratic interests, already thrown on the defensive by this new inequality, are in danger of lapsing further into a national defensiveness that cannot lead to positive achievements.

This issue is complicated further by the fact that the global polity does not just comprise a set of nation states and some weak regulatory institutions. It also contains the USA, which is not just another state but one whose institutions exercise a power going way beyond even that which would be expected given the size of its economy and population. To understand this fully we need to embrace another type of externality: network externality, a concept usually applied to competition among firms. Imagine two firms, each of which develops a similar new product. But one firm also owns the near-monopoly distribution network for the product concerned. The other firm's product does not stand a chance of market success, even if it is superior, as it will be so hard to find outlets. Ownership of the network – 'network externality' – is more important than the quality of the product.

Now apply that to countries. The USA possesses major advantages of network externality:

- The dollar is the sole global currency; as the US administration made clear when one of the ratings agencies threatened to downgrade its credit rating, the USA can resolve its debt problems by printing more dollars, since so many of the world's assets are held in dollars. This is a means of resolving economic imbalances available to no other country in the capitalist world.

- The English language is the sole global tongue. This is not just of enormous business and cultural importance; it also affects scientific reputation. Universities and scientists are ranked according to their performance in certain so-called top-rated academic journals. These journals are all in English, and the great majority are edited from the USA and nested in US networks. Most academic researchers will address some of their work to national audiences, some to international ones. For American (and British, and other Anglophone) researchers this is no problem; for those in the rest of the world it means that part of their work might as well not exist.

- US military power can be exercised almost anywhere in the world, and the special role of armaments in the US economy makes possible many opportunities for state aid to and protectionist approaches to defence-related industries that are not seen as state aid and therefore do not appear to compromise the country's ability to lecture the rest of the world on the importance of free trade and the abolition of subsidies.

- Its mass-market cultural products are recognized and shape fashion and taste everywhere, giving them a strong chance of being preferred to those emanating from smaller national bases, irrespective of their quality.

- The corporations at the heart of its financial sector set the standards by which the world's accounting systems are operated. New York's three financial ratings agencies have become a powerful private form of regulation of governments, and they apply criteria developed according to American perspectives. It does not matter if the products of this system are better or worse than those from elsewhere; the dominance of the US network ensures their success. We learned that lesson the very hard way in 2008 when the US-dominated financial markets proved to be very bad products indeed. But the rest of the world has to put up with them, unless the US government itself were to decide to change the rules. Certainly individual nation states in Europe or elsewhere stand no chance of contesting them.

The advantages of these network externalities help explain the USA's relatively strong economic performance, though this is not a point that will ever occur to economists eager to see in that performance justification for the USA's lack of labour rights and weak welfare state. The international comparisons undertaken in the previous chapter often showed the USA in an extreme position: extreme inequality, extreme weakness of trade unions, extremely low employment protection laws and unemployment pay. It was the only example of a country having such features that also showed strong economic performance. The other countries that shared US institutional characteristics tended to have neither deeply entrenched democratic institutions nor major economic success. Part of the explanation of this US *Sonderweg* lies in its monopoly of so many network externalities.

When corporations benefit from excessive network dominance we look to competition authorities for remedies. But there are no equivalent authorities in the global economic polity that can remedy the subordination to US dominance of the rules of the international economy. We must look instead to the development of alternative networks, so that countries have some choice among them, and so that no one network can dominate the world. The European Union is the main candidate to play such a role, and social democrats have a major interest in developing it in that way. True, the EU was not conceived as a potential rival network to the USA, as at the time of its founding Europeans were heavily dependent on and grateful for US military and economic support. Few, except perhaps in France, perceived the potential implications of this implicit acceptance of US network dominance. However, over the years and largely unintentionally the Union has developed important global networks of its own, especially in fields of competition policy and standard-setting; but it remains a junior partner. And now the situation has become more complex, as there is the possibility of new networks emerging, based on the rising economic powers – China, Russia, possibly even India and Brazil – which can develop their power more rapidly than Europeans, as they start off as existing political units, not as groups of proudly sovereign nation states. They may eventually overtake the excellent start that Europeans had made, and with the possible exception of India and Brazil they are considerably more remote from the values of social democracy than is the USA.

The European single currency has been a major step in the achievement of a global European network presence, and is an example of the sacrifice of national autonomy that is the necessary exchange for being part of a globally effective Europe. But the extent of sacrifice needed was underestimated in the original treaty, because governments were happy to believe the over-simplified economics that said that all the European Central Bank needed to do was to watch over Europe-wide monetary aggregates. Many observers pointed out that this was inadequate, and that sooner or later more detailed monitoring of individual countries' fiscal behaviour would be needed. This time has now arrived. This does not mean that the ECB now needs to impose austerity everywhere. As previous chapters have tried to explain, our principal fiscal and monetary challenge today is not the avoidance of inflation and the control of public spending *tout court*. It is about how public spending and the welfare state are used, about how many nation states can create the social investment welfare state. There is certainly a need to prevent governments from using public debt as a long-term means of financing public spending without having to levy taxes, but there is also a need to encourage properly funded spending consistent with the social investment model. Such an alternative to austerity surveillance means that the monitoring of national government activities needs to go even further than at present being debated in the Eurozone, but the outcome would be a stronger euro, a stronger Europe – and stronger national economies that can avoid both chronic debt and the demolition of important public spending programmes. The alternative is not a 'return' to national sovereignty, but subordination to a global economy dominated by the networks of others, at present and for some time to come of the USA, later from other parts of the world. As we move from a world governed by nation states to one governed by global economic relations, sacrifices of accustomed past habits are inevitable for all. But we do have choice in the kinds of sacrifices we make. The problem is that in virtually no national political forums are the terms of these choices being spelt out honestly and clearly by those who control democratic debate.

The European country that seems most to believe in the continued viability of national sovereignty is the United Kingdom, but, despite the nationalist garb in which the country's Europhobia is normally presented, in reality what the UK actually does is to try to get a share of US network dominance. In some respects it is well placed to do it. The English language originated in England. The UK shares unquestioningly in US military adventures, and in its approach to unregulated financial markets. But it has no co-determination rights in the US polity, except to the extent that some UK-based accountancy firms share with US ones in making the rules that govern global corporate governance. Although only a few people in British politics and banking actually see the issue this way, the choice that the British make by standing on the sidelines, seeking constant opt-outs and threatening to leave the Union altogether, is to sacrifice having a role in shaping a system (as they could do if they participated fully in European institutions) in exchange for passively sharing some components of US network dominance.

Because of the historical origins of the USA as a land of liberty and equality (at least for white persons), its major role in the twentieth century in defending freedom against Nazi and state socialist tyrannies, its role in combating extremist and intolerant Islamic movements around the world, and its continuing prominence as a country in which progressive ideas often flourish (as in the case of feminism), it is difficult for many social democrats to see it as anything other than a benign force. But history moves on. The most important political fact about the USA in the early twenty-first century is that its governing institutions are dominated by corporate lobbies. Even if the Democratic Party is able to win presidential elections with such a figure as Barack Obama, it is itself heavily dependent on funding from corporations and rich individuals. Without their support no presidential or congressional elections can be won. It was notable how President Obama's attempts to reform the financial sector and to introduce improved public health services, two fundamental planks of his original platform, were hopelessly compromised before they were implemented, by opposition running all the way from advisors from financial corporations in the White House itself to corporate lobbying in Congress. The USA will always be in the forefront of moves to prevent action to regulate irresponsible banking or to save the planet from environmental disasters caused by profitable economic activities. It will continue to be a pioneer and world leader in the abolition of the welfare state, the erosion of labour standards and attacks on the rights of trade unions to represent workers' interests. It will continue to have the highest level of inequality in the advanced world, and a regressive system of taxation.

If the USA were just one country among many, these facts (apart from resistance to combating the environmental crisis) would be regrettable for US citizens and for its progressive forces, but not of much concern to anyone else. But, through the dominance of its network externalities and the temptations it offers to other elites, the radical imbalance of political forces within the USA is of importance to all of us. Social democratic values will only be able to advance if alternative sources of global network externalities can be developed. Europe is the only potential acceptable candidate for this – which is why, despite the very strong neoliberal drift in current EU policy, the British right correctly sees European integration as always a potential challenge from the left, a challenge against which the political power of wealth protects the USA. The enhancement of EU-wide network externalities is essential to the construction of the next stage of social democracy; hence the need for a strong euro, fiscal federalism and the transcendence of national autonomy. Meanwhile, however, European capitalist elites are still contemplating how their societies can be made to correspond more closely to the US 'new inequality' model. A struggle for the direction of EU social policy is fundamental to the future of social democracy.

Meanwhile, this dominance of perspectives from one national source tells us something else about the claims of neoliberalism to be the bringer of choice to our lives. This dominance is systematically reducing the diversity of approaches to social and economic problems being pursued in other advanced societies. The market is supposed to provide diversity, but under the pressure of current orthodoxy there is a declining market in approaches to the market itself, no market in markets. This is the opening for a proactive social democracy, in providing alternatives to neoliberal orthodoxy, but still within the context of a capitalist economy. Such alternatives do actually exist and are being pursued in some places in some sectors, but their existence is concealed within the overall orthodoxy. A large part of the process of reviving social democracy lies simply in drawing attention to these alternatives.

References

Butzbach, O. 2005. 'Varieties within Capitalism? The Modernization of French and Italian Savings Banks, 1980–2000'. Unpublished PhD thesis. Florence: European University Institute.
Frank, R. H. 2008. *The Darwin Economy: Liberty, Competition, and the Common Good*. Princeton: Princeton University Press.

Martín, A. and Meardi, G. 2012. *Inmigración, Bienestar y Actitudes ante el Compromiso Igualitario.* Unpublished GUSTO paper.

Standing, G. 2008. 'The ILO: An Agent for Globalization?', *Development and Change*, 39, 3: 355–84.

7

Social Democracy as the Highest Form of Liberalism

The point made at the end of the previous chapter, that social democracy constitutes a major source of alternatives within capitalist society, gives us a sense of *déjà vu* of the labour movement's early years, bringing challenge and novelty to a form of capitalism that had worn out its old tramlines and was being sustained mainly by the fact that the interests it served were extremely powerful. But many things have changed since then. In the early decades social democrats, or socialists as they were then interchangeably called, sought to end the capitalist system, replacing it by various state controls, that would themselves eventually give place to various vaguely defined forms of communal economic management. That vision has today largely disappeared, as the market has demonstrated a widespread capacity to serve many though by no means all popular needs, while state control has shown its very dark side in state socialism, and the further alternatives remain as vaguely defined as ever. As discussed in Chapter 1, social democracy has, over time, come to refer to an approach that uses capitalism and the market, but which, through regulation, taxation, the provision of public services, the representation of the interests of the relatively powerless and a strong representation of employees through trade unions, ensures that capitalism serves a wider diversity of human ends than the market itself can ever achieve. Its claims today to be a challenging, innovative force continue to depend on its presentation of alternatives *within* a market economy, alternatives that are in danger of becoming marginalized as neoliberalism grinds along on its rigid tramlines.

Reflection on a century of European social democracy also reveals its finest triumphs to have occurred when it has ensured both a political and an economic pluralism and inclusiveness, more extensive than anything that could otherwise be provided in capitalist societies. This essentially liberal achievement, rather than state control, should be seen as its hallmark. This perspective provides the basis for an optimistic appraisal of social democracy's future, provided the inhospitable elements in the current and future social environment discussed in earlier chapters can be confronted.

However deficient its future vision, the old socialist left understood the nature of power in capitalist societies better than many social democrats. They saw that the problem of inequality was not just a matter of income differences but an issue of power relations. They could do this because, as Marxists, they believed in the inevitability of eventual transcendence of capitalism; believing that the revolution would certainly come, they did not flinch from seeing everything that was wrong but not amenable to normal political campaigning in capitalist society. Social democrats, in contrast, could see the lack of realism in the Marxists' appraisal of the future, but, needing to believe that problems were amenable to parliamentary politics, they had to see capitalism as essentially tamed and domesticated. This, like the Marxists' dreams, was another escape from realism.

What if we lack both escape routes? What if we believe that capitalist power remains a major bloc to a more just society, but also both that power and its inequalities can never be abolished, while a market economy based on private ownership offers far better prospects than one based on a 'common' ownership that in the end always comes down to state control? If all power is concentrated in the state in the name of the people, it really becomes concentrated in the hands of a small power elite, who will use it to further their own interests and probably to squash opposition. Self-seeking is endemic among power-seekers, and the more power they have, the more dangerous they become. We are always confronted with Acton's famous liberal dictum: 'Power tends to corrupt, and absolute power corrupts absolutely'. Social democracy, as the political movement of the relatively powerless, can never dispense with that essential liberal insight – if only to save it from itself.

Social democracy *does* transcend liberalism, but not in the way socialist thinkers believed. The fundamental meaning of the difference between political right and left is the difference between those who hold established power (the right) and those who are dominated by that power (the left). If the forces that were dominated become the dominant, then the former left becomes the right and vice versa. That was the usual story of the oscillation of power among rival cliques, often through violence, that characterized virtually all pre-democratic societies. This account is slightly over-simplified. There are often groups, which, although not at all part of the established powers, believe fervently in them and the strict order they represent, often wanting them to act further to the right than they find convenient. They are often an embarrassment to the established right, though it sometimes finds them useful. A major historical example was the extreme royalist movement in France of the Bourbon restoration, *plus royaliste que le roi*. Today we find racist populists on the far right, people who are political outsiders but who want established power to exercise a tough authority.

Marx believed that, if the left were constituted by the working class, that cycle of changing positions would come to an end, because the working class was the ultimate dominated class of the mass of the people; its coming to power would then end power relations altogether. But a mass can never come to power. It can only throw up representatives who claim to rule on its behalf, but who then inevitably, at least in part, pursue their own power agenda. The masses of working people remain where they always were. Working people stand a better chance of achieving some political influence when they can exercise choice among competing elites, and where society presents them with a mass of different institutions, than when they are confronted by a monopolistic elite that claims to be their sole representatives, and where institutions that are considered to represent hostile classes have been swept away.

This point is well demonstrated by the political parties that developed historically as representatives of working people: communist, socialist, social democratic and labour parties. When these come to office in a capitalist economy that remains capitalist, the established powers of the society have not been overturned, but there is contestation between an economic elite right and a political left. They may reach compromises, and depending on the nature of those compromises, the political left either retains that position or compromises so far that it becomes indistinguishable from the right. However, when such parties have abolished the capitalist economy, replacing it by a state-controlled one, there is no longer this contestation. The 'left' rules in both economy and polity. But in every case where such a system has lasted for more than a few years, the consequence has been that this left becomes an exclusive and intolerant authority, becoming transformed into a new established right – the process George Orwell captured so brilliantly in *Animal Farm*. We see the final outcome of this in the very confused way in which the terms 'left' and 'right' are used in the former Soviet bloc. Paradoxically, the left can remain the left when it takes political office only when it exists in a position of continuing tension with a surviving economic right.

Since the class of working people can never triumph by collectively gaining control of a political and economic system – in the way that elites can do – societies and polities with strong social democratic movements that co-exist with market economies provide the best available context for protecting continuing diversity and creative political tension.

In the 1950s life in Oslo or Stockholm did not look so very different from that in Prague or Warsaw; austere, limited choice of goods, a stress on collective rather than individual provision, all governed by parties with a strong socialist rhetoric. But the Scandinavians had acquired their model through free elections and open debate; the central Europeans had acquired theirs through military action by the Soviet Army followed by the violent suppression of all rival forces. And these two sets of societies then developed in totally different ways. The former became the most transparent and open societies in the world, with high levels of innovation in the economy and other areas of society. The other became grim police states, with rigid economies and an incapacity for innovation. Nordic social democrats never tried to abolish competitive elections or the capitalist economy; powerful trade unions existed alongside but autonomous from their parties; small, highly open economies were maintained with no protectionism. Some of these conditions, especially the openness of small economies, imposed tough constraints on a strong social democracy that was required to work alongside powerful market forces. The clash produced a high level of creativity in policy development and economic approaches. As we saw in Chapter 5, a form of this combination continues today, and continues to deliver success in the form of the social investment welfare state accompanied by strong, coordinated industrial relations and a vigorous market economy. In a prevailing neoliberal landscape, where many national economies are being pressed into the same mould, with the same capacities and deficiencies, this combination possesses something different that conveys competitive advantages.

This was not how Nordic social democrats interpreted their situation, at least not at first. For decades they believed they were in a struggle to transcend capitalism. They did not advocate centralized collective bargaining in order to ensure that unions came under pressure to take account of general interests and support national competitiveness, as described in Chapter 5; they were seeking to maximize organized labour's unilateral power. But the fact that they were trying to maximize this power in open economies led them, initially unknowingly, to achieve something rather different, but more valuable. Similarly, when British socialists forged the National Health Service that remains the Labour Party's single greatest achievement, they did not envisage the vast collection of excellent medical practices that constitute the NHS today. They shared the general early twentieth-century socialist belief that most ill health resulted from capitalist exploitation, and that once a socialist society had been constructed a national medical system would become only a minor part of public service. Achievements do not always correspond to intentions – even when those achievements are highly successful.

Today, with the advantage of hindsight, we can see what it is that strong labour movements actually achieved, and envisage a future that builds on those achievements rather than on mistaken dreams. A key result of this process has to be the conclusion that, not only can social democracy thrive in a liberal capitalist environment, but in that environment it produces a higher degree of liberalism than conventional liberalism left to its own devices, because it is the clash between liberalism and social democracy that generates the incentive to keep seeking new creative compromises. This is particularly true when liberalism takes its contemporary form of corporation-dominated neoliberalism of the third kind. The contemporary neoliberal economy has become a set of relations between, on the one hand, corporations, and on the other, governments and various kinds of organization, in the course of which citizens are in danger of becoming passive, non-participant users, not party to contracts. Its politicians and intellectuals insist on a dogma about free markets, which destroys diversity and the scope for alternatives, and is applied inappropriately to ignore important market inadequacies affecting working people, but not to disturb cosy relations within the elite itself.

The essential premise of liberalism is that a society of constant challenge, with no enduring hegemonies, produces frequently varying creative tensions from which innovation and diversity emerge. The argument applies in the first instance to politics, where it is associated with the case for constant contestation of embedded elite power and the avoidance of accumulated inequalities. In the economy it appears as the vision of entrepreneurialism associated with Joseph Schumpeter: a process of creative destruction, whereby innovators repeatedly bring together new combinations of previously unrelated elements. From there it is a simple step also to see the argument for liberalism as diversity and disruption in knowledge, including the knowledge needed for public policy.

A key figure here was the philosopher Karl Popper, from the same Viennese background as Karl Polanyi, who, reacting against the tyrannies of fascism and state socialism alike, stressed the imperfection of virtually all human knowledge, even that of experimental science, and therefore the need to keep a permanently open mind, never hoping for certainty, never limiting sources of new knowledge to those with which we are comfortable. Unlike his fellow Austrian and colleague at the post-war London School of Economics Friedrich von Hayek – a major figure in today's neoliberal pantheon – Popper did not interpret the problem of uncertainty as meaning that everything should be left to the market. He insisted on the need constantly to re-examine and revise the theories and knowledge used in both science and policy-making, which implied challenge to market theories along with all others. He called his approach social engineering – a term that he used favourably, but which has subsequently been totally distorted by neoliberal thinkers to describe an approach of top-down, omniscient social reform. Popper meant the opposite; his engineer is the fixer, the piecemeal solver of problems as we go along, coping with life and trying to get on top of difficulties as they appear. Compared with this it is neoliberals who believe they have found a perfect system.

In politics Popper was a social democrat, though one of a very liberal caste. Following the logic of Popper's arguments, Ralf Dahrendorf, one of his most distinguished followers, abandoned his own early commitment to German social democracy and became a Free Democrat, or liberal. For Dahrendorf the pursuit of certainty or utopian states of society was anathema, because the aim of utopianism was to reach an end point where conflict would cease, and where the contours of the good society were fully known in advance. He considered that social democrats had a mind-set of that type, which prevented them from being the friends of constant challenge, diversity and open-mindedness. But he also rejected Hayek and others who sought the pursuit of perfection through the market for the same reason. '. . . [I]f capitalism is a system', he wrote provocatively to a Polish colleague in 1990, 'then it needs to be fought as hard as communism had to be fought. All system means serfdom, including the "natural" system of a total "market order".'

The formal social democracy of social democratic, socialist and labour parties has long ago abandoned the search for a perfect society; indeed, today's defensive social democracy is at the opposite pole of political ambition from that. But both utopian and defensive social democracy are vulnerable to Dahrendorf's charge of shunning conflict and innovation. At the same time, he had no answer to a central puzzle of liberalism: how to ensure that elites do not become entrenched, how to guarantee the social challenges and controlled conflicts that he rightly saw as essential to sustain a capacity for innovation. His own 'liberal' party, the German FDP, has become one of the most committed in Europe to a dogmatic view of the perfection of the market order.

The problem with contemporary liberalism as a political movement rather than as a philosophy is that it depends on a certain balance of forces in society to provide it with the variety it needs, but all it can do is to administer those forces that already exist; it does not produce them itself. Given Catholics and non-conformists, it knows how to generate tolerance between them. Given new middle and working classes clamouring for admission into citizenship, it knows how to welcome them. But by itself it cannot shape which groups will define themselves and so be able to make claims. It is an administrator's politics, which is why in every country liberalism faded into a minoritarian position, unless allied with left or right groups representing more atavistic identities. If the power balance shifts to a position of great inequality and the emergence of hegemonic elites, liberalism has difficulty mounting any social challenge to it – which is exactly what is happening now to Liberal parties across Europe.

In this situation we need a new articulation of the various interests of the mass of people who are not served by present elites, and only social democracy, in alliance with such forces as environmentalism, has the capacity to bear such a mission. Social democratic parties have been better than all other party families in advancing the cause of women and at integrating minorities. They have been more receptive than the centre-right to green issues. Similar claims can be made for trade unions. Very few other mass organizations in contemporary society, with the exception of some religious organizations, have been as successful as they at representing women and ethnic minorities. Social democracy continues to be capable of performing its historical role: to represent those without power within capitalist society, a role which is a permanent one, and without which neoliberalism ceases to be part of the liberal family.

On the other hand, there is much about the adoption of such a role today that does not sit comfortably with historical social democracy, or with either its current dominant defensive form or the direction in which it was taken by aspects of the Third Way agenda. We can see the advantages and difficulties of its position by examining three key areas where challenges must be faced and opportunities arise. Social democrats are invited to recognize both the continuity with their historic tradition represented by the challenges and the need to adjust that tradition to meet them. The latter aspect becomes easier the more social democracy in the twenty-first century can be seen as a joint movement with environmentalists and some other recent radical movements.

Protecting Institutional Diversity

The first is the need to protect economic and social diversity against the dominance of both moneyed interests and the moneyed estimation of all value. Equality used to be seen, rightly or wrongly, as an enemy of diversity; today it is the ally. The idea of economic competition has been reinterpreted in US anti-trust law and neoliberal economics. Rather than describing a situation of ongoing competition among a large number of firms, it can refer to one in which competition has ended in the victory of a small number of dominant corporations. This produces both inequality, giant corporations being a major source of exceptionally high incomes, and lack of variety, as markets become dominated by the few victor firms. The political and social equivalent of this would occur when a particular set of routes to power has succeeded in beating all others; in other words to the historic defeat of all classes challenging domination by the rich. The two aspects, economic and socio-political, come together in the dominance of political institutions by corporate lobbies. In the process, liberalism becomes reinterpreted as corporate neoliberalism and can no longer be trusted to safeguard diversity. Can social democrats, so long associated with a belief in the uniformity of state control, take over that role of defending diversity?

It used to be the political left that threatened the pluralism of institutions in the name of democracy. Socialist orators would complain about 'unelected' judges, whose legal decisions flew in the face of the 'will of the people', as expressed by socialist leaders, who were seen automatically to represent the voice of the people. More recently, socialists and social democrats were very reluctant to see the establishment of autonomous central banks, as these prevented the people's representatives from being able to manipulate certain economic variables in the interests of the people.

Once we transcend the naivety of early views of democratic leaders as the simple expression of the will of the people, we see how dangerous these arguments can be. The very concept of a unitary 'will of the people' uses rhetoric to conceal the deep divisions and uncertainties that exist in any free society. The rule of law has to be protected from interference by politicians, however democratically elected, because interpretation of the people's will is vulnerable to considerable manipulation. It is essential that judges remain unelected. Similarly, it is not in the people's interests for politicians to improve their chances of re-election by pretending that public services can be provided without being paid for through taxation. That route leads to chronic public debt that brings a cost far higher than taxation. An independent central bank can protect citizens from that kind of manipulation by not permitting debt to become chronic. Such actions are not invasions of democracy, but the protection of democracy against those who seek to manipulate it in the interests of their own political careers. Similar arguments apply to the cases for state broadcasting services that are protected from political interferences, and for autonomous government statistical services.

In the early decades of the history of the labour movement the surrounding institutions of society had largely been formed by landed aristocracies and urban bourgeoisies, with both an incapacity and a lack of will to embrace the concerns of working people. In that context championing the 'will of the people' against unelected, elitist judges, central bankers and others was understandable, though the claim that there can be such a unitary 'will' was always flawed. But the context has now changed. Contemporary judges, broadcasters, possibly even some central bankers, have grown up taking universal citizenship and its rights for granted. Indeed, in many countries threats to these institutions are more likely to come from the political right, in its new confidence that the power of wealth to manipulate political opinion enables it to be contemptuous of those important liberal distinctions. In Italy it was the centre-right that allowed Silvio Berlusconi to alter the relationship between the law and elected politicians in the latters' favour, in order to win various personal legal cases. In Greece it was a right-wing government that manipulated the country's economic statistics to facilitate entry into the euro. In Hungary it is a right-wing government that is dismissing judges and civil servants on political grounds, and changing the constitution to suit partisan interests. In the UK it is the Conservative Party that that has been seeking to reduce the number of seats in Parliament in order to suit the electoral geography of its own support. Also in the UK, it is the Conservative Party that complains about the ability of 'unelected judges' to decide issues of human rights.

It is unfamiliar hostile territory for social democrats to become the primary guardians of these independent institutions, but it is essential that they do if society is to be defended against the new power of wealthy interests, which in their confidence are making many attacks on institutional pluralism. It is also necessary to protect social democracy's own preferred policy instruments against abuse, as happens for example when the maintenance of chronic public debt in order to sustain low taxes is passed off as Keynesian demand management. Democracy does not mean that a political authority should be able to do whatever it wants, and it is those who are usually on the wrong side of power relations who have an interest in being protected from power holders' grasp.

Just as there is a need to protect a diversity of public institutions, not just those that are ostensibly democratic, there is a need to protect a diversity of forms of capitalism other than that of shareholder maximization. There are several of these: various forms of mutualism and cooperatives; small firms dependent for finance on contacts with local banks rather than on stock exchanges. They provide a diversity that can be valuable when the shareholder model runs into crisis. But since the 1990s this diversity has been under serious attack from neoliberal lobbies insisting that only the shareholder maximization form can guarantee efficiency. It is ironic that, while the welfare state is often compared unfavourably as offering 'one size fits all' against a great diversity claimed by the market, the market has its own ways of imposing uniformity. In the UK both Conservative and New Labour governments in the 1980s and 1990s facilitated legal changes to enable the country's distinctive form of mutual – the building societies – to turn themselves into normal banks, with control passing from members to shareholders. In the 2008 crisis some of those ex-building society banks were among the financial institutions to suffer the worst; those that remained building societies and therefore under more regulated forms of activity escaped largely unscathed. Accepting greater diversity of forms of corporate organization can be a valuable defence when one form enters a crisis, even if that form has been depicted as the most efficient possible.

Italian savings banks went the same way as British building societies. These had been invaluable in maintaining credit lines to the small and medium-sized firms that are an important part of the dynamism of Italian business in several regions of the country, but they depended on a distinctive form of government regulation. The so-called 'Basel II' process of international banking reform led to the merger of savings banks into conglomerates, in the course of which process local managers lost much of their discretion to grant loans to small firms, and an important resource for a flourishing part of the Italian economy disappeared. One size did not fit all, but all were required to adapt to the one size. The reforms were designed to increase the capital ratios held by banks, which was mistakenly believed to provide an adequate protection of consumer interests, though driven through in a policy-making process dominated by the larger banks. (In the event, this approach proved unable to protect banks from indulging in the speculative markets.) However, Italian governments had some discretion in how they would apply the reforms, and they chose not to intervene. As Olivier Butzbach has shown, diversity in savings banks was protected more effectively in France, though changed and reformed; a country where appreciation of the usefulness of government regulation – on this occasion, ironically, to safeguard local diversity – continues to be shared across the political spectrum.

Responding to the problem of excessive uniformity within capitalism – what we might call the absence of a market in markets – is not an easy task for social democracy. Its earlier preference for state-based uniformity was followed by the Third Way's equally dogmatic insistence on the shareholder maximization model. It is its structural position as an important home for critical opinion and as the representative of non-elite interests, rather than its past policy preferences, that give social democracy this new opportunity. Capitalism today needs more diversity of institutional form. Social democracy is less compromised by closeness to centres of dominant capitalist power than the political forces of the centre-right. It is also more willing to see possibilities for positive state regulation. In many countries therefore it should be in a position to take up this new challenge more effectively than others.

A related area, where social democrats should feel more comfortable in taking action, concerns the re-regulation of the international banking system, an area where there should be scope for creative compromise. At first sight bankers might be expected to want a totally unregulated financial system, as they can then maximize profits without restraint. The rest of the population, which has to pay to save bankers from their mistakes when they produce a crisis, might be expected to want regulation. But on more detailed inspection, should not bankers themselves want regulatory protection from forms of behaviour that have led to them breaking faith with each other, destroying their reputation with the rest of the population and making it harder to trade confidently in the long run? The fact that leading banks manipulated the LIBOR rate – a voluntary market arrangement among banks, not the product of government regulations – suggests that they are unable to police themselves. If these considerations weigh heavily, we should expect to see bankers demanding regulation if only to restore trust to their own relations with each other. We are seeing something of such a reaction in the financial world, but it is subject to three major limitations that weaken its usefulness for true reform.

First, the banks learned from the 2008 Anglo-American bank rescue packages, then from the European conversion of the banking crisis into a sovereign debt crisis, that they will be rescued by general taxpayers from the consequences of their bad behaviour. If they can make short-term profits from that behaviour but will be protected from the consequences of the losses, why should they want to change their ways at all? Second, the leading financial operators have become so separated from the rest of society through their extreme wealth and their globalized detachment from any particular nation state that they do not need to care about the negative reputations they acquire from behaving in this way. If virtually all major banks are involved, we cannot use consumer power to avoid those who have behaved badly; we are stuck with them. (This is another example of how markets dominated by small numbers of giant firms remove power from consumers.) Third, their prospects of short-term gain in the secondary markets are so high that they have a very strong incentive completely to discount any interest in a long term.

It remains in the interests of governments of all parties to take action to regulate banks in order to avoid a continuation of irresponsible market activities, and therefore to do what they can to reorder the sector's incentives so that they are willing to join compromise coalitions around regulation. However, in a globalizing economy individual governments either fear the consequences of losing banking investment to countries with fewer regulations, or themselves want to be among such countries. This leads some of them to join anti-regulatory coalitions with those financial interests that want an unreformed system. The search for productive compromises here between markets and their restraint will depend on groups of governments willing to act for the long term and to find means of punishing those states that try to undermine international regulation. But compromises are not, in principle, impossible. Most interests in complex societies will gain from some combination of marketization and measures to combat its negative consequences, but social democrats should be those taking the lead in organizing international action.

Tackling Externalities

A second major area for future politics is more congenial to social democrats' instincts: taking care of the externalities produced by market activity that neoliberalism ignores. This means seeing where new extensions of the market are creating new problems, and extending the concept of externality from its narrow but still vital concern with issues like pollution. At the same time it is important to concede the economists' case that identification of an externality does not automatically mean that it must be resolved.

An important example is protecting the diversity of human goals. As markets extend further and further, so they lay claim to new areas of life. During the decades of capitalism's first major growth, industrial production presented most opportunities for the extension of markets, mainly in the manufacture of material goods. In a post-industrial society capitalists seek opportunities in the vast and heterogeneous range of 'services' activities, and seek to draw new fields of life into the range of marketable activities. We have discussed above how this provides a major motive for the commercialization of health, education, care and security services. Whether the opportunity for firms to find new profitable outlets in this way should trump concerns over the public service ethos and the problems involved with non-market relations between politicians, public servants and corporations is a question that requires continuous monitoring.

A more difficult challenge in protecting the diversity of human goals that we have already discussed in a different context concerns the division of domestic and paid work. In

Western industrial societies certain areas of life were protected from the market through the gender division of labour: the work of the family, 'women's work', took place largely outside the market (apart from the purchase of products in the market for sustaining the household). The 'commodification of women's work' that has taken place as women have joined the labour force has brought many positive externalities, as it has been an agent of women's political and social empowerment. But there have also been negative ones, in the problems of work–life balance experienced by many 'time poor' families juggling two paid jobs while also maintaining a home and bringing up children, who in turn face increasingly tough competition in the 'education market'. The growth of public-service childcare services in some countries has been a classic example of the major theme of this book: marketization created a problem, public services stepped in to help – whether through direct provision or subsidized private services – and furthered the economy at the same time. But is this as far as we can go in helping families resolve the work–life balance issue? Are there other things that public policy, or agencies in civil society, can do? Or do we accept fraught lives as a negative externality that has to be tolerated, because the commodification of women's work has brought so many advantages?

Workers in manufacturing experience many dangers and often a filthy environment, but they can often detach their personalities from the work activity. This is not the case for those working in personally delivered services: medical personnel, waiters, teachers, shop workers and many others. They have to appear bright and smiling in their exchanges with clients and customers, no matter how they feel and no matter how poorly the clients and customers themselves (also probably victims of work stress) behave. It is a distinctive strain of the services economy, often experienced on top of the exhaustion of work–life imbalance. It is often further coupled to the insecurity and anxiety about potential job loss of people working in a neoliberal labour market with its easy 'hire and fire' regime. One achievement of neoliberalism in several countries has been the removal of discussion of work issues from the political agenda. We have been encouraged to see ourselves as consumers and customers, as investors in financial markets (though few of us are), as users of public services; but discussion of problems for workers is dismissed as special pleading on behalf of 'producer interests'. It is essential that the quality of working life is brought back into political debate, and that this taboo on the subject is broken. Social democrats are better placed than any others to achieve this through their historical association with the labour movement. They also share some of the responsibility for the intrusion of work into the rest of life through their albeit necessary espousal of 'the citizenship of workers' discussed in Chapter 4.

A further example concerns the pursuit of knowledge. Some fruits of knowledge can be effectively marketed: research that is close to the development of marketable products; education and training that prepares, even indirectly, for employment. But if all knowledge generation is closely related to product development there can, virtually by definition, be no truly radical advances. The market cannot demand products that no one knows might possibly exist. Splitting the atom, developing the computer, discovering DNA and later the genome all took place before their vast potential economic uses could be known. They were not initially marketable. Therefore, most advances in fundamental scientific research have been funded by states or by charitable foundations able to operate with criteria outside the reach of the market. In this sense, as Mariana Mazzucato has argued in *The Entrepreneurial State*, states of many kinds have been far more willing to accept risks of failure than private investors, despite the neoliberal doctrine that only the private sector can deal boldly with innovative risk. Generations of politicians have understood this, leading to the concept of academic freedom developed in pre-democratic, non-liberal nineteenth-century Germany, the vast science funding of the US government (despite official US resistance to the idea that state activity can achieve anything positive), the former UK tradition of an arm's-length relationship between state provision of funding for research and selection of the projects to fund. But this model is currently deeply threatened. Under pressure from neoliberal ideology (especially of the third, corporate kind), governments increasingly want to see rapid 'value for money' results from their science funding. 'Value for money' usually means something immediately recognized as useful by a corporation, and corporations feel increasingly emboldened to demand a big voice in how funding is allocated, turning the risk-accepting approach of public funding into their own risk-averse approach.

One sees this very clearly in the EU's science research funding agenda, which has been developed only recently, anxious to please corporate lobbies, and without the historical legacy of recognition of the need for 'pure' science that still has a residual effect on leading national systems within Europe and in the USA. Its programmes are tied tightly to identified corporate or public policy needs. The EU wants to wield its potentially large resources and the vast potential scientific base of European countries to give Europe something resembling the US science edifice. But its research programmes will never develop any fundamental breakthroughs if its agenda remains so close to market concerns (or indeed to governments' existing public policy concerns). Neoclassical economics, from which neoliberalism draws its ideas, is notoriously bad at dealing with innovation and the origination of either demand or supply; it deals with equilibria, adjustment to slight changes in existing states of affairs. For that reason innovation theory looks to unorthodox economic traditions, like that of Joseph Schumpeter, or evolutionary or behavioural economics. When neoliberal policy-making smuggles the orthodox equilibrium approach into a field like science policy, the results are stultifying.

In the same way, under the influence of neoliberalism governments increasingly want school and university courses to be tied closely to the labour market, to give corporations a bigger role in course design and to encourage young people to think of future earnings potential when choosing courses of study. This marketization of education, not in the narrow sense of selling it but more broadly in seeing it as tradable in the labour market, is designed to serve society more efficiently by introducing cost calculations into educational decisions. As with all instances of marketization there are externalities, one of which is a possibly fatal blow to the idea of knowledge as a pure goal in itself: to understand, say, the laws of chemistry or how to read a poem for its own sake, not just a means for use in the market. A pure market economist would argue that, as non-marketable goods, they can have no monetary value set on them, and are therefore by definition worthless; ridding the concept of education of them is therefore a valuable example of how the market relieves us of waste. One can dispute this at three levels.

First, following the above argument about scientific research, one can never know when knowledge that is not immediately useful will one day be so; if we are restricted to knowledge and abilities that we already know to be useful, we can be caught out by sudden change. A small but relevant example is the fact that, when the UK wanted to join the US invasion of Afghanistan, it realized that almost no one in the UK could speak the Afghani languages; that kind of useless knowledge had been driven out by an early batch of reforms designed to make education 'relevant'.

Second, it is essential in the general struggle against neoliberal hegemony that we assert that many things that cannot be marketed do have real value to our lives, and that we will fight to protect them. If the enjoyment of pure knowledge is treated with contempt, then love (except for its bogus form as prostitution), the appreciation of beauty (except at commercial beauty spot tourist sites) and laughter (except at comedy shows) will all go the same way.

Finally, there is a great danger in encouraging young people to see education mainly in terms of access to very large incomes. Only a very few will achieve these incomes, and most will have to settle for something more modest. Unless they can also see their education as something that gave them access to stores of knowledge that they love and possess for their own sake, they will be embittered.

These examples by no means exhaust the list of issues where contestation of market externalities and inadequacies in the interests of promoting the diversity of goals of human life must take place. There is a strong temptation to want to protect such things by placing them on some basis of rational calculation, beyond value judgements, either to complement or to rival the claims made on behalf of the market for being able to achieve that goal. For instance, there are frequent attempts to use cost–benefit calculations to determine whether the advantages that might flow from building a new rail or road connection are outweighed by the environmental damage that it would cause. One can make some progress in this way, and such measures should be taken as far as possible, but at a certain point one has to accept that the evaluation of some costs goes beyond elements that can be translated into monetary terms. For example, how does one evaluate damage done to natural beauty, where it is impossible to charge persons for going to observe the beauty spot? Unless we accept the actually existing market prices as the only means of assessing human values – which means denying the existence of externalities – we cannot escape making value judgements and bringing these to bear in political conflict. That is the struggle between the first and second forms of neoliberalism that we have to accept – and learn to welcome warmly – as a source of continuing diversity and innovation in a liberal and heterogeneous society.

Cynical political observers will say that very few people outside churches and universities really care about non-material values, and that politicians need to stick to bread-and-butter issues. But few successful politicians heed that advice themselves, virtually all making use of moral appeals at key points of their campaigns. It might be argued that all this is mere rhetoric. For many of the politicians involved it might be, but they would only bother to use such rhetoric if they believed there was a public out there wanting to hear it. This is perhaps nowhere more true than in the USA, the country that sometimes appears to have gone further down the road of materialism and shareholder value than any other. Controversies over religion, the treatment of the human embryo, patriotism, community activism and identity are at the heart of US politics. It is just that issues of the morality of the market, especially the labour market, are sidelined in these debates. If it has been possible to mobilize a large nation around the issue of abortion, it should be possible to do the same about how the babies who are born are eventually treated when they grow up and enter the work force. There are opportunities here for social democratic politicians to use, and they connect them to a rhetoric that belongs to them more than to others, and to their own heartland.

The 'Common Good'

Finally we reach the special cases of those externalities that are embodied in a common good and either cannot be reduced to a sum of individual goods or, although ultimately reducible in this way, cannot be achieved by individuals acting without coordination at a higher level. The second of these situations is more easily considered, and will be discussed first.

There are many cases where we should like to act in a 'good' way, but fear that if we do so, advantage will be taken of us by those acting in a 'bad' way. A bank might want to offer accounts to people with poor debt records, and it might calculate that it could afford to bear the cost of those who eventually default on their debts, provided that it bears only a proportionate share of them. But if it is the only bank offering such a facility, it will attract all bad-debt accounts, and its profits will sink below those earned by all other banks, which refuse to accept any bad debts. This could result in the collapse of the bank concerned. Or a clothing firm may want to raise the wages it pays to very low-paid workers stitching jeans and T-shirts for it in Bangladesh. A substantial improvement could be made to those wages while adding very little to the price in Western shops of the final product, so small a proportion of final costs is represented by these workers' wages. But if the firm is the only one doing this, that small change in its final prices might be enough to lose a large amount of trade to rivals who continue to pay starvation wages.

One solution to such problems is for all firms involved to agree together to accept the bad debts or to raise the wages. But this runs into two problems. First, unless the market concerned contains only a small number of firms, it will be difficult for firms conforming to the agreement to do anything about those who remain outside it, and there would be many advantages in staying outside. Second, such voluntary arrangements – especially if they seek measures to impose sanctions on those not abiding by the arrangement – are likely to be in breach of EU competition law. Competition law recognizes the completely free market alone as the source of any good; if a goal, such as helping people with poor credit records to gain access to banks, or lifting starvation wages, cannot be secured through free competition, then competition law has to regard it as a bad objective. Only political action can release us from moral straitjackets of this kind.

More general is the problem of real collective and public goods, goods whose consumption cannot be individualized, or collective actions against bads that cannot be individualized. Even here the goods and bads themselves are experienced by individual persons. We care about damage to the environment, climate change and biodiversity because these affect the lives of millions of individual human persons (or indeed, in some instances, individual dumb animals). Social democrats and liberals, including neoliberals, share this fundamental humanist position, but it is not universal. For example, some forms of Christianity and Islam consider that the goal of human action is to celebrate God, this being superior to any implications it might have for human life. Communists elevated a collective class to an importance quite separate from the fate of its individual members. The 'individual' of market economists is a calculating automaton very removed from the passions and feelings of actual human beings; indeed, a giant corporation can be treated as an 'individual' in economic theory. Some environmentalists seem to perceive the planet as something that we should care about quite apart from the sentient life on it. In the same camp are appeals to patriotism or a great cause that project the *patrie* or the 'movement' as an entity standing over and above the mass of people who comprise it. It is notable that such abstract collective goals usually become personified in the person of one individual, a monarch or a revolutionary leader. Those of us in the liberal humanist tradition should be extremely suspicious of any appeals to collective goals that cannot be reduced to the felt experiences of actual human persons (and possibly other animals). That still leaves some differences between goods that are immediately and obviously individually enjoyed and those where our enjoyment has to be shared, but the sharing still takes place among persons who experience the goods as individuals.

Shared goods suffer from problems of trust. In order to make the sacrifices needed to achieve a collective good (sacrifices like losing some of our income in taxes), we have to believe that we shall receive our share of it, or that those who we are willing to help with it will receive their share. We may not even be sure what that share is. And there is the familiar collective action problem, that it is difficult to exclude free-riders, who have made no contribution to achieving the good, from enjoying it. This may make us both wary of contributing ourselves and wanting to be among the free-riders. Issues of this kind are particularly important in an increasingly interdependent world, where our capacity to damage each other's social and natural environments has become so extensive. This is classic social democratic territory and a set of issues where no other political movement (apart from Greens) is so well equipped. But it is also vulnerable territory because of the problems of trust.

We discussed in Chapter 2 the paradox of how the working class – historically the 'private' (or 'deprived') class, excluded from consideration of society's collective needs – became the custodian of collective goals. The paradox happened because workers' private resources were so small that they needed collective action where wealthier people could make private provision. This changed with the arrival of a predominantly affluent working class that could fend for itself provided the tax burden was kept low. This has become the great Achilles heel of social democracy. How does a population rise above seeing politics in terms of immediate personal interests? By the 1990s this had become a major problem in all democratic polities, especially with the market economy seeming to offer so much that was tailor-made to individuals' needs, able to dispense with the trust problem that bedevils collective action. In general, parties across the spectrum responded by turning the issues at stake in elections into market-like individual choices: 'your' school, 'your' hospital, 'your' police force. The fact that public business is necessarily about larger, collective questions, which, though touching individual lives just as much, cannot be reduced in this way, was concealed from voters. As a result voters' capacity as citizens was undermined. What seemed to be a recognition of their individual freedom was ironically really a return to treating them as deprived persons not capable of embracing anything beyond immediately perceptible individualized interests: the neoliberal model of citizenship.

The history of winning the right to be political citizens, the right to vote, is largely a matter of groups excluded from citizenship coming to perceive and resent that exclusion, and therefore struggling collectively for inclusion: classes, members of religious minorities, the defeated in civil wars, ethnic groups, women. In many cases (though in general not that of women) that collective awareness, including an awareness of which political movements supported admission and which opposed it, remained with the groups concerned and helped form their collective political identity for well over a generation. Ironically, they were bound to the social whole by identities that often expressed their previous exclusion from that whole. But once people have become accustomed to being citizens, the identity that had served as their badge of entry declines, and there remain just individual citizens coming to terms with a political class divided into parties. These then appeal to them in terms very similar to, and indeed based on, the way adopted by competing producers of goods. How does a population with established citizenship rights, which are increasingly defined as analogues to commercial products, come to take that citizenship as seriously as one in search of those rights?

It was the rhetoric of marketing that led us up the cul-de-sac of the purely individualized framing of issues. A change of rhetoric could help people see those cases where they can achieve their individual goals only alongside others; the goals themselves can remain individual. In any case, a very broad swathe of public opinion does care about many of these collective goods: urban and rural environments, decent public institutions and mass media. But this does not mean making bland appeals to a general national collectivity, as though there were no conflicts of interest within a nation, or as though somehow people outside the nation constitute a kind of opponent. Political parties do seem to find it easy to identify internal opponents of the collective good when these latter are weak and unable to fight back, such as immigrants, or people dependent on benefits. The 2008 crisis and its aftermath have made it far clearer to many, perhaps a majority, of people, that rich and powerful elites can threaten their interests considerably more. In most European countries it has become possible again to talk about the problem of inequalities, and to criticize the behaviour of banks, private firms delivering public services and other corporate interests. This provides an opportunity to dismount neoliberalism from its dominance of public debate, and demonstrate how individual ends often need to use collective means.

Rising to the Challenge

There is a tricky problem for social democrats as they define their new role, in that neither private property ownership nor the state are reliable defenders of the rights and freedoms of an open society, as they both thrive by constantly extending their range of control, and dominant groups within both will try to pursue their own interests despite the incentives that markets and democracy, in their different ways, give them also to serve public ends. Delivering a task to the social democratic state no more disposes of a problem than leaving it to the market. Openness, innovativeness and diversity depend on the gaps and spaces that exist around and between states, corporations and other major organizations – the spaces that they cannot capture, but which are inhabited by the active, critical groups of civil society.

This is an arena of repeated struggle. During the industrial and student revolts of the late 1960s and 1970s there was considerable debate about the problem of 'ungovernability', a claimed lack of necessary order among modern, non-deferential populations. Social democrats did not contribute much to that debate, which started as a conflict between the far left and conservatives, but became one between conservatives and neoliberals. Conservatives were anxious about incipient anarchy. Neoliberals redefined the new search for freedom from order and control as a search for freedom within the market, which is itself a highly controlled space. 'Shut up protesting and go shopping!' was the implicit popular message of 1980s neoliberalism. In the 1990s the message was amended: 'If you cannot afford to go shopping, have some unsecured credit.' In this way the doctrine that started life as 'monetarism' – reasserting order by ensuring control over the supply of money – became associated instead with irresponsible private money supply (the banking crisis), leading to popular revolt against banks, fiscal restraint and capitalism in general. We have now come full circle and the issue of ungovernability is on the political agenda again. Can democracy be made safe for capitalism? – a question often asked in the 1970s – reappears as the call for *marktkonforme Demokratie* (market-conforming democracy).

We need not fear for the ability of authority and power to regain control after every outbreak of unruliness. The bigger question is the following one: an open society depends for its innovative strength on the inability of powerful institutions (mainly corporations and states) to keep things under their control; that is, on the existence of occasionally unruly, truly public spaces. But public spaces are vulnerable if no one has the job of protecting them. Who can be trusted with this task, if not states and other large institutions? The answer is that these institutions are needed as agents for the task, but never as its principals. Groups of citizens never lose their responsibility for caring for parts of the public sphere that is important to them, and must therefore retain a willingness and capacity to monitor, criticize and mobilize. In Chapter 2 I described how a range of groups across the British political spectrum mobilized to oppose privatization of the public forests. They seemed, oddly, to be content to trust the government that wanted to privatize the forests to maintain them. What they in fact trusted was their own capacity to monitor and criticize that government if it misused the forests, a capacity that they feared they would lose if the forests disappeared into private ownership. This example concerned a literal case of 'space', but a similar logic applies to a range of abstract spaces, from scientific research to political protest. If we trust either the market or the state, it is when we believe we can trust that they are so organized that they leave us our own capacity to monitor, criticize and mobilize against them.

The lesson from this for social democrats is that they should never allow their movement, their party, their unions to be absorbed into supporting the state so fully that it obliterates those important spaces. Neoliberals of good will should believe the same about the market.

References

Butzbach, O. 2005. 'Varieties within Capitalism: The Modernization of French and Italian Saving Banks', 1980–2000. Unpublished PhD thesis. Florence: European University Institute.

Dahrendorf, R. 1958. 'Out of Utopia', *American Journal of Sociology*, 64, 2.

Dahrendorf, R. 1990. *Reflections on the Revolution in Europe: In a Letter Intended to Have Been Sent to a Gentleman in Warsaw.* London: Chatto and Windus.

Mazzucatto, M. 2011. *The Entrepreneurial State.* London: Demos.

Popper, K. 1945. *The Open Society and its Enemies.* London: Routledge and Kegan Paul.

Schumpeter, J. 1942. *Capitalism, Socialism and Democracy.* London: Routledge.

8

What About the Party?

A book of this kind will be expected to have paid more attention to political parties. I have deliberately avoided doing so, since their normal occupancy of centre stage distracts the attention of political commentators from deeper structural phenomena that shape policies and politics, to which I have wanted to devote most attention here. The identity of governing parties is only one of the factors affecting the pattern of policies that emerge at particular times and places. Governments in Paris will always seek more regulation of financial transactions than those in London, even if the former are Gaullists and the latter formed by the Labour Party, because for complex historical reasons a strong role for the state is shared across the French political spectrum, while the British economy depends heavily on the activities of the City of London. Bourgeois governments in the Nordic countries will always maintain stronger welfare states than Democratic administrations in the USA, because historical experience of the welfare system has been highly positive in that part of Europe, while corporate lobbies on behalf of wealthy interests who do not like paying taxes dominate Washington. I have wanted to depict the struggle between different political approaches as taking place at deeper, more resilient levels than electoral campaigns based largely on advertising slogans.

A second reason for not concentrating on parties emerged at the end of the previous chapter: while the state, and therefore parties, are necessary to the achievement of social democratic goals, they are not sufficient. No political leaders deserve the trust implied in the idea that one delegates to their charge issues about which one cares deeply. Similarly, one has not discharged one's responsibility to a cause in which one believes solely by supporting a party that includes that cause somewhere in its programme. Social democracy has to be a movement more extensive than a party, and social democrats need often to join with people with different party allegiances or none in campaigns. This is actually good news for citizens who want to play a part but do not want to stand for election or climb a party hierarchy. You do something for social democracy every time you engage in a campaign against a negative impact of marketization (say, a campaign drawing attention to the terrible working conditions of garment workers in the Third World, or seeking to limit the exposure of young children to television advertising), or championing a cause neglected by market-driven processes. These last could be issues as ostensibly remote from each other as claiming some land for community activities rather than private development, or protecting the pursuit of a cultural or scientific project as a goal in its own right. The same happens every time you pay a subscription to a trade union or do something to encourage union membership. At least, that is the case for social democracy in the role I have assigned it as the principal force for combating the extremes of neoliberalism of the first and third kinds.

Seen in these terms, the scope for contributing to social democratic action and doing something to civilize the on-going business of marketization is very widespread, open to masses of people in their daily lives, and not just something to be confined to small groups of politicians, their advisors and academics. Some people will object that in doing some of the things I have listed they are not being social democratic at all, but following a religious belief, just being a responsible citizen or even just doing their job. This is not a problem. Cause organizations, whether political, religious or whatever, have a choice whether to regard themselves as broadly based and as part of movements wider and more amorphous than themselves, or to insist that they are the only true representatives of a narrowly defined project. The approach taken in Chapter 7 necessarily commits me to the former view, against narrowness and orthodoxy, against knowing in advance that one is right, but always willing to accept new insights from surprising places. I have presented neoliberalism of the kinds I find unacceptable as drilling down deep into our society with a sharp and narrow focus. To contest it we do not want a movement constructed on similar lines, as orthodox Marxism or radical Islam can provide. A central part of the case against neoliberalism is the need to stress the diversity and uncertainty of human ends and means, and this needs to be mirrored in the way that the conflict is organized.

Finally, in avoiding day-to-day party issues I have wanted to explore the scope for developing the historical legacy of social democracy in ways that will make it relevant to today without being tied down to existing party programmes or the problems of individual nation states. I have therefore been concerned with policies, their types and goals, rather than with electoral politics.

It is, however, far more likely that governments including social democrats will pursue these causes. Therefore the issue of parties has to be addressed. The approach I have adopted in previous chapters does not embody a fatalistic structuralism devoid of actors. Lobbies representing wealthy interests, ensuring that international finance is not regulated or that public services are contracted out to favoured firms on soft terms, have been very busy around these pages. So have harassed trade union leaders, seeking ways to improve their members' lives without prejudicing firms' competitiveness. In the background too have been many vigorous groups drawing governments' attention to what they see as

the negative externalities of various aspects of marketization, and being contested by those trying to show that the
marketization in question will favour the general interest.

However, while I have been clear about the moneyed
power base of neoliberalism, I have been vague about what
constitutes the power resources of social democracy, apart
from trade union membership. I have talked about inequalities of class power, but it is not clear whether degrees of
inequality are the causes or the consequences of policies.
They are of course both. Where levels of inequality are low,
the ability of wealth to translate itself into political power is
that much reduced, and therefore policy outcomes are less
likely to reinforce those inequalities, and so on; the structure
of society and policy outcomes interacts mutually in a self-
reinforcing way. But if wealthy and corporate interests are
working hard the whole time to articulate that interaction
to their advantage, social democrats cannot just leave matters
to work themselves out, as I am in danger of having just
described.

I have also argued that an important strength of social
democracy is its need to internalize the confrontation between
the imperatives of the market and the imperatives of goals
that are ignored or crushed by the market, as in the example
of trade unions reconciling members' needs with competitiveness. But, as we saw in Chapter 5, unions act like this
only when they are structured in certain ways. And, looking
beyond unions to the mass of campaigns that I claim form
part of the wider social democratic family, most of these face
no such constraints at all. A group campaigning to protect
a local environment against construction of a new railway
line does not have to balance the need for the line against
the need for the local environment. There have to be points
where these conflicts are worked out, and if social democrats
regard that as someone else's concern, they condemn their
movement to being only a mass of protest groups.

These arguments lead us to the normal case for political
parties which seek to become governing parties, where they
then take on these difficult roles. They have to articulate the

overall demands of campaigns and causes, while also reconciling conflicts, both among these and with the needs of the
market. Given that parties that have been the historical carriers of social democracy exist, usually as one of the two
biggest parties, in all western and most central European
countries, it would seem that we have reached a satisfying
resolution of the problem of agency: Carry on as you were,
social democratic parties! But there are severe problems with
believing that this is possible, which we must now address.

Confronting the Declining Electoral Base

First, the electoral base of social democratic parties, like
that of historical conservative and Christian parties – there
is no difference between left and right here – is shrinking.
Parties are losing their traditional social roots among declining pre-industrial and industrial classes and religious communities, while the ordinary working populations (rather
than the economic elites) of post-industrial societies still
fail to generate stable new political identities. This leads all
parties to adopt a catch-all approach, seeking voters anywhere and everywhere. In such a search, clear identities of
any kind are a handicap. This is not so much a problem for
the centre-right, as the moneyed interests that it principally
serves provide a superbly solid and unwavering sense of
direction for the day-to-day conduct of government, leaving
the parties free to say whatever is necessary for mere electoral purposes. It is more difficult for social democratic
parties, which lack any such equivalent power source, and
are in grave danger of wandering away from any clear social
anchor to a sense of purpose. This occurred very clearly with
the Third Way social democratic parties, which often ended
by trying to share something of the centre-right's links to
private and corporate wealth.

However, it is possible to argue that a political identity of
normal working people in post-industrial society has been
formed, but not fully recognized as such. The biggest single
difference between the industrial and the post-industrial

work force, at least in the Western world, is that, whereas the former was very predominantly male, the latter has a majority (though not an overwhelming one) of female workers. And advancing women's interests has been a major achievement of democratic politics of the past thirty years. Further, whereas in industrial society majorities of women voted for centre-right, particularly Christian, parties, in most of Europe today they are more likely than men to vote for social democratic and green parties.

One cannot quite claim that feminism is the new social democracy. There is a neoliberal interpretation of feminism, to the extent that feminism stands for the marketization of women's work. There has in fact been a shared neoliberal and social-democratic agenda here, against conservative interests. Also, of course neither social democracy nor any other major political movement can become feminist in any sense of being 'anti-male'. However, there are elements of a feminist agenda where neoliberals cannot follow social democrats, as we see already in the role of childcare policies in the social investment welfare state, and which do not raise the problem of being hostile to men's interests.

The social democratic politics of industrial society was male-dominated, but this did not make it 'anti-female'; what it did was to interpret women's interests in a male-oriented way, as in unions' demand for recognition of a 'bread-win-ner's wage', i.e., a wage that would enable a man to support a non-employed wife and the children for whom she was caring. There is scope today for a politics that interprets everyone's interests, including men's, from women's perspec-tive; not 'anti-male', but embracing within it men's equal, but less easily expressed, demands for a balanced life. As dis-cussed above, classic industrial society 'protected' certain areas of life from the market by keeping them in the home, where relations were supposed to be conducted according to different rules. Contemporary marketization has broken down much of that protection, liberating women and chil-dren and drawing them into the market – for women the labour market, for both women and children the consumer market. But this liberation comes at certain costs, as marketization always does: for example, the commercialization of leisure and of childhood, or the effect on family life of extended working time that we have discussed. There are potential political issues here. The barrier between family and market having been brought down, politics is bound to enter too. Childcare policies are an important start, but probably not the end, to a post-industrial politics that takes the family and its relationship to the working world seriously. Historic male perspectives accompanied a politics of industrial society where home and family were the remote concerns of women, churches and church-linked parties. Post-industrial society brings us different configurations, based on women and their less compartmentalized approaches to life moving centre stage. This is all promising material for social democracy. It presents possibilities for constructing identities, based on but not limited to women's life experiences, that link problematic daily encounters with marketization to the wide public issues of how to cope with its negative externalities. If we are all to be workers, probably to work longer hours, and to work until later into our lives, usually in work roles that require us to engage our personalities, we shall need to bring the problems of working life to the political agenda, alongside our concerns for health, education, care and security. Trade unions already exist as the channels for doing this, provided they can see the opportunities and persuade far more working people than at present that they can plausibly take on the task.

Tackling Labour Movement Weaknesses

Second, I have here described a certain kind of trade union movement as particularly favourable to social democracy: one that is broadly representative of the work force – encompassing all key sectors, and in particular private services – and so organized that it is heavily constrained to accept the need for competitiveness. Such movements exist in most of the smaller western European countries and in Germany, but not much elsewhere. If unions do not have those character-istics, they face one of the following fates: they become too weak to achieve much (as in most of central and Eastern Europe); they protect a declining minority while being unable to do much for the bulk of the work force (as is threatening to happen now in Spain, but soon in the Nordic countries too); or they become powerful but without a capacity to use that power in a way compatible with a well-functioning economy, even if their leaders want to do so (as sometimes occurs in Italy and used to occur in the UK before the unions were weakened). The implications of this problem are enhanced by the fact that, under the pressure of both neo-liberalism and occupational change, unions are everywhere losing the characteristics associated with compatibility with strong social democracy. It was this situation that led Third Way social democrats to want to cut their links with them. The implication of that, however, is to cut social democracy off from the main point of organized contestation of neolib-eralism, off from the world of work as a source of social issues, and off from virtually the only institutions in contem-porary society run by and for normal working people. All constitute part of the trap that lured Third Way social democracy ever further into the corporate and neoliberal embrace.

The model of unionism discussed in Chapter 5, simultane-ously working for employee interests and accepting market constraints, appeared at one time to be a special feature of the Keynesian period, when the main challenge was to ensure that government guarantees of full employment did not result in inflation. That whole approach seemed to lose its rationale when governments abandoned the full employment guarantee, and exposure to the rough edges of the market and fear of unemployment seemed to governing elites to be a far more congenial substitute for responsible unions. But in Chapter 5 we saw the continuing vitality of that form of unionism in today's new imperatives of negotiating paths not around inflation, but between marketization and its inadequacies and negative consequences. Social democracy should not want at all to lose links with a force like responsible unionism that can help with those negotiations. Rather, it could use more organizations of that kind, where they exist – such as cooperative, mutual and consumer movements. There is a deal to be done between social democratic governments and trade unions – and I do not think that it can be done without such governments. Unions need more rights and powers to be able to represent the interests of workers in private services and in unorthodox forms of labour contract. Only in that way can they avoid the trap of representing a declining, ageing and relatively privileged minority of the work force. In exchange for those powers they need to adopt structures that will require them to accept a search for means of reconciling their members' needs with the search for competitiveness. This includes making the 'flexicurity' switch in their approach to employment protection: placing less emphasis on protecting workers in existing jobs, and more on supporting them strongly in their moves around the labour market.

What this search means in practice will not be the same everywhere. For countries of northwest Europe already launched on the social investment welfare state and competing economically on the basis of skills and rich infrastructure, the challenge is only to restore a position that is slipping. The situation in France, Italy and the UK is different. These countries are partly on the way to the social investment state, though in different ways, but their trade unions are not well structured for playing coordinating roles, and in the UK they have been excluded from public policy for three decades. But these are remediable problems. For parts of southern Europe and for most of central Europe outside Slovenia, the challenge may be too steep, and the opposite, unattractive path of seeking competitiveness on the basis of price alone seems unavoidable. A major shift in the orientation of public spending towards the creation of a skilled work force and high-quality infrastructure would be needed to lift some countries out of this path. Others in central Europe have elements of this in place, thanks to certain positive aspects of the Soviet legacy; though, thanks to that same legacy, their unions are rarely in a strong position to participate in the process.

The situation in southern and central Europe might at least seem to offer social democracy the chance to pursue its old simple agenda of building a basic welfare state and labour laws, and to some extent that did take place in southern Europe after the fall of fascist regimes, and in central European countries as they accepted the limited social policy agenda that accompanied EU entry. But the route through 'competing on price' is increasingly difficult. Today in many sectors this means wages and working conditions competing with the far lower ones in the Far East. Social democrats in these European countries need even more than others a degree of transnational regulation of labour conditions, such as through the introduction of ILO standards into the rules of the WTO. Paradoxically but understandably, parts of their populations are responding in exactly the opposite way, seeking an escape from globalization in xenophobic movements. This brings us to the challenge of building a supranational social democracy.

Moving Beyond the Nation State

Finally therefore, and most difficultly, social democracy has to move beyond the nation state. The historical base of all democratic political parties has very firmly been the nation state. This gives them all a strong incentive to draw power to that level, away from both more local and supranational levels. Social democratic parties have been no exception to that, as the edifice of the welfare state in whose construction they played such a major part is determinedly national. When social democrats (and others) talk about 'universal' benefits, or the need for 'everyone' to have the same chances of access to services and better life chances, their universe and their sense of everyone stops at the national frontier. Further, one exception to the declining social bases of political identity discussed above is ethnic nationality. Partly because other such bases have declined, partly because of the tensions of globalization, right-wing xenophobic, racist and anti-European parties have gained strength in virtually all countries. This is leading other parties to stress their commitment to the nation and to adopt a defensive pose in favour of it against foreigners of various kinds.

I have tried to show, mainly in Chapter 6, that the nation state is no longer an adequate vehicle for monitoring marketization – and implementing effective policy responses – in a globalized economy. The attention of citizens has to be shifted to politics at higher levels, not in order to grab back to the nation state business that is being conducted at those levels, but rather to strengthen supranational institutions and to encourage citizens to develop a democratic politics at those levels, since many issues can be confronted only there. This is again a special problem for social democratic and for other left and green parties, because those of the centre-right can leave much of the business they want transacted supranationally to be carried out by transnational business interests, while hypocritically draping themselves in national flags.

A supranational democratic politics does not require citizens to identify with these higher levels, only that they respond positively to electoral programmes and civil society movements that call for action there. A sense of national community is too important to the legitimacy of the welfare state, not least in the Nordic countries, for social democrats to want to risk moving too far beyond it. But that in no way excludes stressing the dependence of national welfare states on supranational protection. The same is true for many other important areas of policy. For example, at present the debate over transnational regulation of the financial sector takes the form of some parties claiming that they will take measures at their own national level, while others say that only supranational action could work, but that this would be impossible, so therefore nothing should be done. What we need is for parties to boast that they will work together with other governments for action at EU or global level. It is what they know they have to do – and often do do – in practice, but the advantages that seem to flow from banging a purely nationalist drum mean that they only rarely talk to citizens in those terms. But this argument depends heavily on shifting the EU and the European Court away from their present stance of attacking national social policy through ever wider extensions of competition doctrine. This requires a campaign for policy change at the EU level and international party collaboration – not an attempt to escape from the European level.

At the same time, in many countries there is a need to move decision-making to levels below the nation state. Historical social democracy was a distinctly centralizing political force, in the tradition of French Jacobinism that in the eighteenth and nineteenth centuries accurately perceived local and rural interests as bastions of conservatism against modernizing and democratic pressures. It became part of that suspicion of all interests outside the tight ranks of the labour movement criticized in the previous chapter. The tradition was strengthened in post-war Europe, when the Catholic Church, fearing being swamped by a secular coalition of liberal and socialist forces, stressed the idea of subsidiarity – decision-making at the most local feasible level – as a means of defending its loyal, local communities. This brought social democrats and socialists to identify even more closely with the nation state. But as the history of the Church itself – in earlier centuries the most important centralizing force across the whole of western and central Europe and beyond – shows us, major social interests very rarely have a permanent preference for centre or locality, or even need to have such a preference. Just as some social democratic interests today require supranational institutions, others require greater localism. This is especially the case where marketization represents the interests of transnational capital pitted against locally important interests and values.

9

A Feasible Prospectus?

I began this book by arguing that social democracy in most European countries needed to snap out of its current defensive posture and become assertive. There is certainly no need for social democrats to feel that their movement's work ends with the decline of industrial society. Alongside green movements, they are the only political force that specializes in requiring capitalism to fit itself to the wider needs of society. (Nationalist and racist populist movements give the impression of being critics of capitalism, but, just like their fascist and Nazi predecessors, their reform agenda is limited to punishing the foreigners and minorities who are in reality the system's principal victims.) Social democracy has a larger agenda in the early twenty-first century than at any previous time, as capitalist business activity, seeking new opportunities for profit following the decline of manufacturing industry, is intruding more pervasively into areas of life that it previously left untouched. In addition to needing to provide political parties capable of dominating elected governments, social democracy can today draw on masses of citizens' actions that share this central goal. These reinforce the role of parties, and can to some extent substitute for them when their electoral fortunes are at a low ebb.

While the classes that supported social democratic parties have declined with industrialism, the parties have potential access to important new forces generated by post-industrial society. In Chapter 8 we have looked briefly at the scope for politics to continue to reposition issues around women's perspectives. Chapter 7 did not consider who in the population might be the carriers of social democracy as a force for innovation and questioning, but it is a role most easily borne by younger generations. Neoliberalism and social democracy have both been well placed to seek new core constituencies among women and young generations, as forces of traditional conservatism, that kept the former in the home and required deference to authority among the young, decline. Neoliberalism offered both groups the freedom of the market, but that freedom came with costs. Neoliberalism has already squandered its potential among women through its rejection of the social agenda and public services that reconciliation of life in the market and in the home requires. Its promise of individual market freedom made a more promising start among the young, but it becomes increasingly clear that this freedom requires as a *quid pro quo* submission to managerial domination and acceptance of insecure contracts in working life.

Social democracy now stands better placed than its rivals among these crucial groups, though only if it is understood in the sense I mean here, of a movement and set of ideas that include political parties but extend far beyond them. I have argued that parties and unions both need to and can afford to relinquish the tight and centralizing mentality that dates from their earliest decades, when they were surrounded by a hostile society. It is unlikely that the new generations of post-industrial society will ever accept the kind of disciplined political behaviour that traditional parties used to assume. Modern parties need to accept loose and varying alliances, and social democrats more generally need to see their political action as taking place in a variety of different life fields, not just politics in the strict sense. This is a positive development that enhances the capabilities of all of us.

There is another reason for welcoming a looser, less loyal, relationship between parties and the wide circle of their supporters: we can never quite trust political and other organizational leaders not to betray us. This is particularly true for movements of the left, where Robert Browning's famous attack in his poem *The Lost Leader* (1845) on William Wordsworth has been echoed in every generation:

> Just for a handful of silver he left us,
> Just for a ribbon to stick in his coat –
> Found the one gift of which fortune bereft us,
> Lost all the others she lets us devote;
> They, with the gold to give, doled him out silver,
> So much was theirs who so little allowed:
> How all our copper had gone for his service!
> . . .

All movements are healthier when supporters approach leaders with scepticism and constant monitoring, unless trust has been thoroughly won. The best way to avoid disillusion is not to have illusions in the first place, and this is easier to do when a movement has not placed all its eggs in the one basket of its leader's (or leaders') performance. Well-intentioned leaders should respect and see the value of this; in the societies of the future it is likely to be all they can expect. This is why social democracy now needs to welcome becoming the centre of an often troublesome and disobedient but creative and honest extended family of campaigns and movements.

This book has not aimed to set out a shopping list of specific policies, but to point out general policy directions. This is particularly necessary when I want to stress that the social democracy of the future needs to be far more extensive than an organization grouped around a manifesto and an electoral programme. However, some fairly clear guides to policies and actions – variously for parties, campaigning organizations and concerned individuals – do emerge. The following examples from three policy fields indicate the policy implications that flow from the general stance; readers can try applying a similar logic to others.

Markets, Regulation, Public Services

Nearly all social democratic and even socialist parties have by now abandoned the idea of a socially owned or state-owned economy and accepted that most goods and services will be produced by private firms. But that leaves scope for considerable policy-making. Some of the general themes proposed in this book for a revived social democracy (welcoming the role of markets but being alert to their negative externalities; seeking the creative possibilities of diversity; and distinguishing between true markets and corporation-dominated ones) provide several guidelines for constructing detailed policies. First, the idea, so dominant in the 1990s and 2000s, that the Anglo-American shareholder-maximization firm provides the best possible form of capitalism needs severe re-examination in the wake of the financial crisis, in particular its corollary that short-term asset values on stock markets served as the best possible measure of a firm's value. Other forms of accounting and of corporate structure exist and have had good records, until the rise of the secondary and derivatives markets seemed temporarily to out-perform them. Some of these alternatives, such as financing with debt capital and bonds, as well as forms of mutualism, are better suited to such activities as industries with long-term research and development needs, or the organization of pensions. Facilitating these is one of the ways in which social democracy, as a source of alternatives within capitalism, can encourage a diversity that standard neoliberalism rejects. Similarly, space needs to be protected for small and medium-sized enterprises and the diversity they bring to products and services. Competition policy needs to take a tougher line in limiting the monopoly power of large corporations; a potential consensus point between neoliberals of the first kind and social democrats.

Second, many markets need regulation. Neoliberalism is ambiguous about this question. On the one hand deregulation, 'cutting red tape', 'getting the state off the backs of enterprise', have been major slogans of neoliberal politics. On the other hand, the 'regulatory state' is often seen as neoliberalism's alternative to social democracy's state control. Nearly always when formerly state-owned enterprises have been privatized, a regulatory agency has had to be established alongside it, because these industries usually remain monopolies or oligopolies. The purpose of neoliberal regulation differs, however, from the regulation usually seen as 'red tape', because it limits its activities to trying to make firms behave as they would if they existed in more perfect markets. This usually means regulation of prices and aspects of the treatment of consumers. This is a very sound starting point, but it is possible to go further, to consider consumers' interests more broadly, and to take account of externalities. This too is sometimes done, as for example when there are environmental restrictions on where electricity firms can locate overhead pylons, or when energy firms in general are obliged to advise customers on energy efficiency, contrary to their own interest in maximizing sales. This whole policy area is one where conflict and compromise among my three forms of neoliberalism can be seen in action. Pure neoliberals of the first kind will want regulation to concentrate on creating markets alone. Those of the second, social democratic, kind will be concerned to add important externalities to the regulators' brief. Corporate neoliberals of the third kind will be wining, dining and in other ways capturing regulators so that they operate with a light touch and a blind eye.

Regulatory capture needs to be guarded against, offering a role for the campaigning, watchful extended family of social democracy, since politicians of all parties are very vulnerable to becoming implicated in such a capture. But campaigning groups can do more in relation to regulation. There is often truth in the neoliberal charge that regulation becomes 'red tape': rules that have lost their purpose, but which go on creating burdens for businesses (and perhaps jobs for some public officials), and also discrediting any valuable goals the regulations originally had. We see this particularly clearly in the field of health and safety, where excessive, unthinking caution can lead to absurd rules that threaten to undermine some very real issues. Such situations are often the result of an all too often experienced sad life cycle of campaigns. A group campaigns with vigour and dedication to remedy a real problem; success is eventually achieved with the introduction of new regulations, and the campaign fades away; implementation is passed on to an administration that understands nothing of the original struggle, but implements the regulations in an unimaginative and bureaucratic way; the regulations, and therefore the original real issue, become discredited. It is very difficult for government machinery by itself to do anything about this kind of problem, because it is itself a cause of it. Only continuing interest by groups in civil society with a passionate concern can do that. This is a major reason why campaigns and citizen's actions must never be seen as subordinate to and replaceable by action by governments.

Finally, a commitment to seeking diversity in organizational forms needs also to check the now almost universal assumption of contemporary policy-makers that the quality of public services will be automatically improved if they are privatized or contracted out. This thinking has become so dominant that the European Commission refuses any more to speak of 'public services' but insists on 'services of general interest'. Behind this lies the belief that the market always ensures superior delivery. But, as has been argued in earlier chapters, that is likely to be true only where there are markets with real competition. Most cases of privatizing public-service delivery do not provide that, but hand services over to corporate power, which is not a synonym for the market. There is often room for serious debate about whether public service or market competition more benefits users; both are likely to be preferable to provision by a non-competitive corporate political favourite. Privatization or the outsourcing of public services should only be attempted where there are clear possibilities of gain for ultimate users through choice. The losses that come through excessive closeness between public officials and corporations offset some of the other gains that might seem to come from privatization and outsourcing without competition. If governments want, as well they might, public services to benefit from efficiency gains that have taken place in the private sector, they can better do it by hiring private-sector managers in public service. If they want private-sector finance for infrastructure projects, they might do better to issue bonds rather than to privatize. If they want competition in public service delivery, it is often possible to organize this among units within the public sector.

There is also a deeper point here. In his trenchant critique of the dominance of economic ideas over human life, *Homo economicus*, Daniel Cohen argues that some of the most desired commodities in post-industrial societies, such as education, health, and some aspects of information technology, neither need the market for efficient delivery, nor are necessarily well delivered by the market. It is certainly the case that extraordinary steps are being taken by governments to impose a corporate market model on schools, universities, hospitals and other health care services that has not been historically present, and which does not easily fit. Similar acrobatics are being performed in order to create an artificial scarcity and therefore a market for cultural and informational products that can otherwise be made available at no cost on the Internet. As the only major political force not completely committed to the corporate neoliberal model, it is up to social democrats to explore the scope for both new and historical forms of delivery of services of this kind.

In sum, the general thrust of marketization should not be opposed as a matter of principle, but a sharp eye needs to be kept on the various inadequacies of the market and the damage it sometimes causes. These, whether they harm customers, workers or the third parties typically touched by such externalities as environmental damage, provide much of the stuff of twenty-first-century politics. Groups who are negatively affected naturally look to politics for a remedy. Social democrats cannot assume that they will always want to support complaints against the market, but they are well placed to champion good causes among these. What constitutes a 'good' cause cannot be spelt out *a priori*; working it out has to be left to political debate and struggle. The point is that, if everyone except committed neoliberals vacates the field, no such debates and struggles can take place. In recent years this has become a particularly rich area, as campaigning groups have identified such issues as the use of slave and child labour in multinational corporations' supply chains, the use of ingredients harmful to health and also the depletion of natural resources in commercial food processing, and a wide range of other environmental issues. This new politics involves campaigns directly targeting corporations, sometimes leaving aside governments and parties, and raises important ethical questions.

Social Policy and Taxation

The welfare state has become a sorry victim of neoliberal propaganda, and many social democratic parties have adopted 'me too' positions rather than contest the hegemony. Rather than a set of citizens' rights, embodying our membership of a national community that cares for us at times of difficulty and weakness, the welfare state is depicted as a device for transferring money from people who work to those who refuse to work, pretend to be ill or come into a country as immigrants solely to join these other idle groups. Social democratic politicians can never win a competition with the political right to amass the greater number of distortions of the role of the welfare state, and they would be better engaged pointing out how many of us, or those close to us, can become innocent victims of economic fluctuations and other of life's disasters, and might need some of the services of the welfare state at some time.

More productive, but equally challenging to the neoliberal stereotype, is the task of transforming existing welfare states so that they conform to the social investment welfare state model. This – provided it is combined with the equally important policy of providing generous income replacement during periods of unemployment if workers are to be expected to embrace labour-market risk and change – can become a major trademark policy approach for social democracy, linking its historical roots to the requirements of a modern agenda. Family-friendly labour policies are central to this. The approach also includes policies for infrastructure, including: those directly related to current productive needs (such as road-building and training); those that form part of the role of the entrepreneurial state, more adventurous and risk-bearing than most private-sector activity (such as research); and those that improve the urban living environment.

The key theme here is the role of strong public policy in mediating with markets, enabling them to operate and even enhancing them, while protecting citizens against the disruption that they can cause. In earlier chapters the policy implications of this in the labour-market field have been analysed in some detail. Similar exercises could be carried out in other areas of social policy. One such example would be local economic development. This is an increasingly important area for economic policy, as cities and regions seek ways in which they can become hosts to firms and other organizations that can provide employment and economic activity in the new global economy. De-industrialization has brought particular crises to areas once characterized by a small number of manufacturing activities. Responding to this with new solutions is a key area for public policy, enhancing infrastructure capacities and work skills. There is, however, here, as in other fields, a strong tendency at present for corporate neoliberalism to take over. Local development authorities develop close relations with a small number of large corporations, who might open a plant, a shop or other facility. Local firms, community groups and unions tend to be left out of the process. As a result there is a decline in locally based entrepreneurial capacity, the area becomes excessively dependent on a small number of large firms, who can dictate terms to the local authorities, and the High Street is dominated by the same universal store chains as everywhere else.

Social policy and other public actions necessarily require financing through taxation; financing through chronic public debt is no alternative. This is often seen as a major political vulnerability of social democracy. If elections become auctions to cut taxes, then clearly neoliberal parties are at a permanent advantage – unless they are pursuing expensive military agendas or needing to engage in exercises like the recent bank rescue. Taxpayers' revolts have been predicted since at least the 1970s, when critics first began to announce that the Nordic welfare states had reached the limit of taxpayers' tolerance. Forty years later the Nordic countries and some other northwest European countries continue to maintain tax rates considerably higher than those in the USA. Of course, it is not possible, desirable or necessary for taxation levels to go on rising, and plateaux need to be reached; but attempts to find the maximum taxation levels that populations will tolerate have not been successful, mainly because different national polities differ so much. An important variable is the perceived effectiveness of public spending and whether many citizens trust that their taxes are being used in ways that they consider valuable. This places a premium on ensuring efficiency, as well as reliably providing services that are seen as valuable by local populations.

A further aspect of social policy discussed in particular in Chapter 5 was the restoration or establishment of strong trade unions and other forms of labour representation, with extensive coverage across the whole work force, with approaches to membership that meet the needs of the new precarious part of it, and with structures that pressure them to work alongside rather than against market forces. This is a major area for both social democratic parties in government and for the wider left-of-centre community. Government action is probably needed to offset the threats that employers can make, especially in the private services sectors, to prevent workers from joining unions, and generally to handicap union activities. But no one wants a state-dependent union movement; so this is a signal for widespread social action. This is particularly the case for temporary workers, and workers in various kinds of false self-employment. Unions neglect them at their peril, but orthodox approaches to membership are probably not appropriate for them. As part of this the new stresses and miseries of working life need to return to the political agenda, so that they rank alongside problems of consumption and the use of public services. Many of these stresses are not the results of personal problems and inadequacies, but of bad work organization and unreasonable and authoritarian management. They are therefore questions of public importance.

Transnational Politics

Most difficult of all, but highly important, is to bring policies for governance and regulation, including taxation, at European and global levels into the heart of democratic debate. It has been made clear at several points in preceding chapters that the national level is in no way adequate for achieving the regulation of a globalized economy. Not only do international transactions require international governance, but at present corporations exercise a political blackmail by threatening to remove themselves to countries where regulation is lighter and taxes lower. It is not that there is no activity at the international level; there is a good deal of it, and governments engage in actions together around these issues almost every day. The challenge is to bring national democracy to bear to support European and international action.

The crisis, which ought to be making the need for international action blindingly obvious, is having the opposite effect on many on the political left. This is partly the panic response of '*se sauve qui peut*' that one must expect to see in a crisis, though panic serves no one's best interests. In Europe it is partly a response to the extreme neoliberalism of the EU's response to the crisis in southern Europe. Social democrats both there and in northern Europe are starting to argue that they need to get more autonomy from Brussels in order to stand a chance to develop social democratic responses to the crisis. But autonomy from the EU does not bring autonomy from the global stock markets, corporate investors and ratings agencies who are the primary agents of neoliberal policies – unless one also embarks on a protectionist track, which is what some on the left in Greece and elsewhere are now starting to propose. This has to be resisted, as has already been discussed.

Social democracy has never thrived in protectionist economies, which are dominated by politically favoured business elites and/or dictatorial state bureaucracies. Strong social democracy has always been associated with free trade; some of the reasons for this were explored in Chapter 5. But for the essentially neoliberal free trade environment to be compatible with social democracy, it has to make possible neoliberalism of the second kind – that is, to possess means for tackling market inadequacies, negative externalities and a need for public goods – at the level at which the free trade operates. Today this means the world. This does not mean that the world has to be subject to a single social democratic regime, but that means must be available for achieving some degree of global regulation. As was discussed in Chapter 6, such means do exist today, but they are weak. The challenge for social democrats is to strengthen them. For activists in civil action campaigns, such as those around supply chain labour abuses or tax evasion, this is already an important field of action. The weakness is with the parties. These need to change their rhetoric to take pride in their efforts to achieve goals in cooperation with other counties, not in their national separatism.

This applies particularly strongly at the level of the EU, where so much can and needs to be done to combat the current neoliberal hegemony. The most straightforward means of democratizing the EU and encouraging parties and governments to work constructively would be a formally very simple rule that said that the Commission should be elected by the European Parliament and not nominated by member states. That would transform the Commission into being a government of Europe and would lead parties of all kinds to develop serious cross-national programmes and to take elections seriously. This will not happen, because national governments so enjoy their power of patronage in appointing commissioners, and being able to point out that the Commission lacks the democratic legitimacy that they possess themselves. But it is in the substantive political interest of social democratic (and some other) parties to place the simple proposal on the agenda, as without that it will never even be debated.

Grounds for Optimism

It is easy to make the case that this new social democratic agenda is unrealistic. Neoliberalism retains both its ideological hegemony and its sheer power in the form of corporate wealth and unregulated financial markets. Against that I propose pitting social democratic parties with declining core electorates, similarly declining trade unions, and a motley assortment of environmentalist and anti-corporate campaigners. To many this will be reminiscent of the Polish cavalry charging German tanks in the Second World War. But defeatism of this kind becomes merely another part of the neoliberal hegemony, another way of arguing that 'There is no alternative'. It is essential to try to get beyond this and to consider neoliberalism's various points of vulnerability.

The extent of its ideological dominance is often exaggerated. This can be examined by returning to my identification of three kinds of neoliberalism. The first kind, the pursuit of pure markets, constitutes the form that is considered to be ideologically dominant. It seems to embrace all the ideas of freedom of choice, low taxes and individual liberty that are at the heart of the US Tea Party thinking, and which so many on the left still seem to fear is unstoppably attractive to voters, despite its defeat in the 2012 US presidential elections. It is important fully to register the fact that in no democracy does a major party subsist on policies based solely on neoliberal ideas. Parties that do so, for example the German Free Democrats or the Dutch Liberals, remain small. Parties that seem to be both large and neoliberal will always be found to accompany their neoliberalism with other ingredients that are, on a strict analysis, incompatible with it, but which render the party more popular than could possibly be achieved by the neoliberal agenda alone. Christian democratic parties and the US Republican Party accompany their neoliberal elements with values based on religion, tradition and community, which are not compatible with the primacy of the market as the only source of value that is at the heart of neoliberalism of the first kind. More secular conservative parties also retain appeals to traditionalism and nationalism (as in Estonia and the UK). If British New Labour, US New Democrats and Scandinavian bourgeois parties count as neoliberal, they have achieved political strength only by combining neoliberalism with elements of social democracy.

By itself pure neoliberal doctrine is too intellectual to mobilize masses. It can be popularized through slogans about individual freedom, but that is only half the story of the market. The other half is discipline and constraint: the market allows us to satisfy our individual freedom to the extent that we can do so by using the market alone. If we want things that we either cannot afford or which are not available in the market, or which the market will destroy, then we cannot have them. Economics used to be known as the 'dismal' science, because it taught the lesson of scarcity and constraint – choice as the need to have some things but go without others. Part of the ideological triumph of neoliberalism during the 1970s and 1980s was to remove all emphasis from this side of the picture and to stress freedom of choice only in the sense of being able to have, ignoring the need to go without that which is not chosen. But the limited reality of what markets can give us cannot be concealed, and pro-market, neoliberal ideas always need to be accompanied by the other ingredients discussed above.

Advocates of the third kind of neoliberalism, corporate neoliberalism, rarely dare to speak openly of their preferred model – though the current British government has come fairly close to this by producing a formal list of large corporations that are members of what it calls its 'buddy' scheme. These firms are assigned a minister in the government to whom they have privileged access for lobbying purposes. Originally, in 2011, thirty-eight firms were part of the scheme; since then twelve more have been added, and there are plans for thirty more during 2013. Occasionally, an individual corporation will claim boldly that its monopoly position is in consumers' interests, and of course general product advertising does much to give giant corporations a popular friendly image that they would not enjoy if the public saw them just as vast accumulations of wealth and power. But no major political movement is likely to see championing their cause as the high road to mass popularity, even if many like accepting their money. Far more widespread is the concealment of neoliberalism of the third kind behind that of the first kind.

This leaves the second, essentially social democratic kind: widespread use of markets where possible and useful, but a willingness to check, regulate and offset their effects where they threaten to destroy some widely shared goals and values, and leave others as unattainable. Most of the alliances that neoliberals make with other forces express precisely that kind of compromise, whether it is with religious, nationalistic, conservative or social democratic values. But it is social democracy itself, especially if allied with green movements, that most explicitly and within itself expresses that compromise between the market and checks on its interference with other values. Of course, the range of these 'other values' is vast and they do not together form a coherent package; and hard choices remain. But the crucial point is that, if there is a diffused hegemonic ideology around neoliberalism, it is not around its rather arid and uncompromising pure form, but around a reasoned and balanced correction of it. The recent changes in the approach to markets of the IMF, OECD and World Bank are part of this process of balanced correction – a process that has been reinforced by recent very widespread revulsion at the behaviour of global finance, that behaviour having been the purest expression of the combined force of neoliberalism of the first and third kinds against the second.

If neoliberalism of the second kind is expressed as: 'Let markets work for us, yes; let them tyrannize us, no!' it provides a powerful rhetorical base, and in more sober form it provides a rich and promising political agenda. In parading it social democrats – whether active in parties, unions or other causes – need have no fear that they are voicing unpopular minority concerns. They stand foursquare in the centre of public opinion and political reality.

The problem lies not with ideology but with the power of the interests that benefit from neoliberalism of the other kinds; in short, the power of capital. This power is partly embedded in globally mobile finance capital – which is why international political cooperation is so fundamental, and one reason why it is so difficult to achieve. But it also operates at national and local levels through the funding of political campaigns, ownership of mass media, resources for lobbying, the ability to purchase the best brains. It would be foolish to claim that these are paper tigers. The globalization of capital and associated growth of inequality have in some respects returned us to the imbalance in class relations typical of the late nineteenth and early twentieth centuries, where politics serves the interests of a small elite. There are two major differences, which stand on either side of that balance. On the one hand there is not today a rising working class seeming to present a major threat to established power. On the other hand we live in societies with extensive rights and openness, and with populations that are not deferential but critical, suspicious of authority, sometimes unruly, whose votes are needed by politicians, and whose consumption is needed by firms. It is because of these changes that opposi- tional politics takes such a different form today, with a greatly reduced role for solid mass organizations and a greatly increased one for a mass of different campaigning activities, including consumer movements directed at corpor- ations as much as at governments.

The international campaigns of 2012 that proposed a con- flict of interests between a top one per cent and the remaining 99 per cent raised such a division for the first time in decades within advanced societies. Divisions have normally been pro- posed between middle class and working class, or between everyone else and minorities of welfare claimants and immi- grants; divisions that in no way question that one between the real power holders and the rest of the population, the one that threatens the legitimacy of those power holders. If opposition to their behaviour becomes widespread, they will be forced into compromises. These will be unsatisfactory compromises, because the power imbalance remains so uneven – the '99 per cent' will never unite. But if we talk ourselves into believing that nothing can be done, join no campaigns, unions or parties, we can achieve no compromises at all.

At present the most serious challenges to the neoliberal order are coming from the populations of Greece, Spain and elsewhere in southern Europe, where there is real fear of both civil disorder and the sheer inability of people and institutions to cope with the shock to living standards, employment chances and public services. It will not be pos- sible for authorities to meet these problems with the repres- sion of past decades, even if in Greece and Spain those decades were as recent as the 1970s. There will have to be compromises. Unfortunately the southern European protest- ers have to defend a social model that provides no base for a future dynamic economy, but which is all they have; and they are concentrating their rage against the EU or the German government, who are allowing themselves to stand in for the banks and the 'markets' that should be the real focus. One can rarely choose where important social battles have to be fought. But that only makes it more important that challenge and criticism are extended across broader fronts. 'They', the established powers, need us: to work, to make purchases, to vote, generally to behave ourselves even though we are no longer deferential; and to do these things willingly. They can be made to pay a price to regain this willingness.

References

Browning, R. 1845. 'The Lost Leader'.
Cohen, D. 2012. *Homo economicus*. Paris: Seuil; in English 2014, Cambridge: Polity.

Index

Page numbers in *italics* refer to a table